Cecille Crow
march 5, 1989

TIFFANY
GLASSWARE

NORMAN POTTER · DOUGLAS JACKSON

CROWN PUBLISHERS, INC. NEW YORK

Published by Crown Publishers, Inc.,
225 Park Avenue South, New York,
New York 10003
First published in Great Britain in 1988 by Pyramid, an imprint of the
Octopus Publishing Group, Michelin House, 81 Fulham Road, London SW3 6RB
CROWN is a trademark of Crown Publishers Inc.
Printed by Mandarin Offset in Hong Kong

Library of Congress Catalog Card Number: 88-47888

ISBN 0-517-571234   10 9 8 7 6 5 4 3 2 1   First American Edition

CONTENTS

My family at Somesville *by Louis C. Tiffany, 1888*

Chapter One

EARLY INFLUENCES

The son of the New York jeweller and silversmith whose shop is still a byword for elegance, Louis Tiffany was a many talented man whose wide-ranging artistic achievements were matched by equally brilliant entrepreneurial skills. He was first a painter and then an interior designer before turning his full attention to the art glass which was to bring him his greatest fame. The seed was sown when, as a young man, he visited Europe, North Africa and the Middle East and fell under the twin spells of the medieval stained glass windows in Europe's cathedrals and churches and the long buried ancient iridescent glass which archaeologists were unearthing.

In particular the sale was a triumphant vindication of the creativity and craftsmanship, and above all the artistic integrity, of a man who through his art glass almost single-handedly created an American version of the essentially European Art Nouveau movement.

Around the turn of the century Louis Tiffany was designing and making his glass for the finest houses in America, including the White House itself, and for some of its greatest public buildings. From vases and lamps to tiles and stained glass windows, his work formed the basis of sumptuous interiors for the workplaces and homes of the fabulously rich merchants and industrialists of America – 'an extravagant people, leading extravagant lives'. Tiffany himself was one of them, the son of a wealthy jeweller and a larger than life character who set himself up as an arbiter of taste, decried the American propensity for importing art objects from Europe and set out to create a truly American version.

For some 40 years the Tiffany studios and glassworks produced a vast range and quantity of decorative and useful objects for both the American and foreign markets. By the turn of the century he was employing more than a hundred craftsmen, but despite the volume of production Tiffany never allowed himself to lose sight of his artistic ideals, and every item was guaranteed to be of the finest quality.

Above: *Louis C. Tiffany in middle age*
Opposite: *The shade of the Magnolia lamp which made a record auction price*

When a magnolia leaded glass and bronze floor lamp by Louis Comfort Tiffany fetched the astounding price of $528,000 (then £436,364) in Christie's New York rooms in March 1985, it was dramatic confirmation of the complete renaissance of late 19th and early 20th century Art Nouveau, after its decline following the First World War and its 'rediscovery' in the 1960s.

Sadly, he lived to see Art Nouveau both flourish and wither. Tiffany himself died a bitter man, appalled by the new 'modernism' — the stark functionalism that replaced the sensually elegant, flowing and natural forms of the style he did so much to create. Like that of many of his artistic contemporaries, his work was dismissed as outmoded, even faintly ridiculous, and his vast output became an object of public indifference and critical derision. Stunningly beautiful Tiffany lamps, vases and other supreme examples of the glass-maker's art that had once sold for hundreds of dollars, were auctioned off for a few cents each or, unsold, consigned to the rubbish dumps of New York. Many of Tiffany's great stained-glass windows and mosaics were destroyed by once enthusiastic owners who now considered them far too ostentatious and theatrical for practical day to day use. His interiors in many a fine house and apartment were dismantled, their contents dispersed, and the decor redesigned. For Tiffany it was the end of an American dream.

Reappraisal

The re-emergence of Art Nouveau has brought about a timely reappraisal of the work of this elegant American, whose own background and lifestyle were no less colourful and flamboyant than the objects he created. In museums and art galleries around the world Tiffany glass is being presented as among the most beautiful creations of the Art Nouveau movement, and certainly the most outstanding art glass produced in the United States. It is eagerly sought after by collectors and commands high prices, both for its artistic merit and its rarity.

Many thousands of pieces of Tiffany glass were destroyed. Fortunately many still remain, in private and public collections, often in the unlikeliest of places. The largest collection outside America, and in terms of quality one of the finest in the world, is not as you might expect in London or Paris, Rome or Vienna, but in the small Lancashire town of Accrington, in the northwest of England. It was a gift to Accrington by a son of the town, Joseph Briggs, who in 1890 when aged only 17, went off to visit America for three months but instead joined the Tiffany company and lived for the rest of his life in New York.

The organization that he joined was by then reaping the rewards of the success it was to enjoy until well into the 20th century. Tiffany had turned his dreams of creating an American version of Art Nouveau into reality; his reputation as an interior decorator had taken him into the homes of the famous, from Mark Twain to the President of the United States; and his early experiments with glass had led to the formation of the Tiffany Glass Company in 1885. Yet this was only the beginning, for after 1890 the newcomer Joseph Briggs was to witness the growth of the Tiffany companies to greater and greater heights; and he himself was to play no small a part in that growth.

***Opposite:** This tulip shaped flower form glass vase, made circa 1900, stands 34 cm (14½ inches) high*

His employer, Louis Comfort Tiffany, was born on 18 February 1848 into a family that could trace its American ancestry back to 1660 when Squire Humphrey Tiffany settled in Massachusetts Bay colony. Louis' father Charles Lewis Tiffany (1812–1903) was, and perhaps still is, the most famous Tiffany of all, the man who founded the world-renowned jewellery company that still bears his name.

Charles Lewis Tiffany served his time in the family's general store in Connecticut but in 1837 at the age of 25 he borrowed $1,000 from his father, moved to New York and in partnership with a college friend John Young opened the modest stationery and fancy goods store that they called Tiffany & Young (later to become Tiffany & Co.) at 259 Broadway. From the start their 'fancy goods' – carefully chosen and lovingly displayed artistic items from around the world – attracted customers searching for the exotic and the beautiful, and the reputation of the store quickly spread. The partners imported the finest wares from Europe, from Bohemian glass and Dresden china to clocks and bronzes. They also began to design and manufacture their own brand of silverware, of a quality high enough to be hallmarked.

French Crown Jewels

Charles Tiffany used his own particular love of jewellery to build up a fine collection of gems. Tiffany & Co. imported jewellery from Italy, France and England and in 1850 acquired a collection of diamonds once owned by Marie Antoinette. By 1887 the firm was wealthy enough to buy a large portion of the French crown jewels for two million French francs, and they also obtained the largest yellow diamond ever mined.

By the time Louis was born Tiffany & Co. were jewellers and silversmiths to millionaires, and some of New York's most influential families, among them the Vanderbilts and Astors, the Goulds and Havemeyers, were patrons. The company soon achieved international fame, with impressive showrooms in London and Paris.

By all accounts Louis Tiffany was a wilful child but with a fine sense of aesthetics. Brought up in a household packed with beautiful objects, he could also scarcely ignore the fine craftsmanship that was being carried out in his father's workshops. In particular he came under the influence of Edward C. Moore, the Tiffany company's master silversmith and a connoisseur of the arts, who taught many of New York's young artists and craftsmen to step outside the familiar world of American and European art and look to the more exotic cultures for guidance and inspiration. All this had a profound affect on the young Tiffany and few were surprised when he decided not to enter the family business but instead become an artist.

The formal approach of art school did not suit Tiffany's character and after

Opposite: Three iridescent glass vases and a magnificent iridescent glass plate

graduating from Flushing Academy, Long Island in 1866 he spent a year sketching endlessly in Manhattan, while studying informally under the landscape painter George Inness, an American working in the Barbizon style and a fine teacher, particularly of technique and composition. The young man's talent was obvious and within that year he had

the leaders of a Paris school that practised Oriental art. It was under Bailly's guidance that he first began his 'grand tours', slowly wandering and sketching through Moorish Spain, travelling to North Africa, visiting Gibraltar and Egypt, Venice and other Italian cities, Tangiers and Bohemia. In London he almost certainly met and conversed

a painting chosen for the National Academy of Design. In 1867 he used his father's business connections in London and Paris as a pretext to visit Europe, and here he found an art world that had become fascinated by the exotic styles of the Middle and Far East.

With Edward C. Moore's influence still strong upon him Tiffany entered into this world with relish and for a year or so studied under Léon Bailly, one of

Above: Sow with piglets, *a water colour by Tiffany, circa 1900*
Opposite: *The Last Judgement, a window from the Cathedral of St Michel, Brussels which was made in 1528*

with the leading artistic intellectuals of the day – among them William Morris, Rossetti, Burne-Jones and fellow American James McNeill Whistler who had made England his home.

For several years Tiffany travelled about Europe, North Africa and the Middle East sketching, painting with a new-found love of watercolour and studying architecture and design. These journeys made a strong impression on his creative sensibilities and years later he told the Rembrandt Club of Brooklyn:

> When first I had a chance to travel in the East and to paint where the people and the buildings also are clad in beautiful hues, the pre-eminence of colour in the world was brought forcibly to my attention. I returned to New York wondering why we made so little use of our eyes, why we refrained so obstinately from taking advantage of colour in our architecture and our clothing.

Tiffany had a lifelong love of glass as an artistic medium, beginning with an early interest in the great mediaeval artists whose glorious stained-glass windows adorn Europe's cathedrals and churches. His admiration for their use of coloured glass matched his dislike of later painted windows and he determined that one day he would emulate the mediaeval masters. Now, on his travels, he added to his fascination for glass and its use for both practical and decorative purposes. This was a time when archaeology was changing from a rich man's pastime into a science, and excavations throughout North Africa and the Middle East were giving an astonished world the first glimpse for hundreds and sometimes thousands of

16

years of the long-forgotten arts of antiquity.

To Tiffany the ancient glass unearthed by archaeologists was a revelation and he soon amassed a sizeable collection. He was particularly captivated by the astounding colours and textures inherent in the material. After lying buried for long ages many of the glass objects had decomposed or had been affected by metallic oxides in the soil, and their flaking surfaces had taken on a pearl-like quality in delicate shades of blue, green and gold. Sometimes their surfaces were rough and pitted, but to Tiffany even this added to their attraction.

Perhaps subconsciously at this time he recognized that many of these ancient glass pieces were artistically *complete*: neither etching nor painting would have improved them in any way. It was a philosophy he was to apply throughout his glass-making career and despite the appalling technical difficulties that this presented, Tiffany seldom resorted to additional ornamentation of his pieces.

Samuel Bing, the influential Paris art dealer and critic, whose 'Maison de

Opposite: *A Roman glass pitcher with a mould-blown body, dating from the 5-6th century AD, which was found near Tyre in the Lebanon*

Right: *This green glass Roman amphora, which was made in the late 7th or early 6th century BC, has the iridescent surface, acquired from being buried in the earth for many centuries, which Tiffany admired so much*

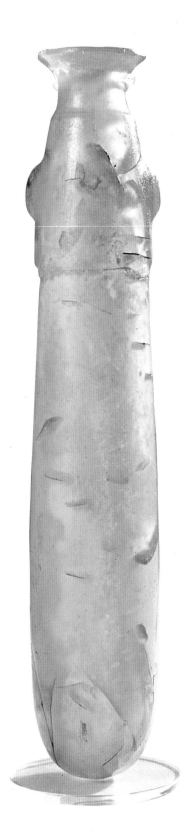

L'Art Nouveau' gave the entire genre its name, was a close friend of Tiffany and introduced his work to Europe in the 1890s. He once pointed out:

> If we were called upon to declare the supreme characteristic of this glass-ware, we would say that it resides in the fact that the means employed for the purpose of ornamentation are sought and found in the vitreous substance itself, without the use of brush, wheel or acid. When cool, the article is finished.

Tiffany had gone to Europe to further his career as a painter. He returned in 1870 with a much more ambivalent attitude to the subject, for his horizons had broadened considerably. He had been exposed to the decorative qualities of Islamic and Oriental art; he had embraced the teachings of William Morris and the English Arts and Crafts movement; and he had begun to think seriously about the techniques of using glass in decorative art.

Such a patchwork of ideas and interests did not make the choice of a career a simple one for Tiffany. Rather like the colours on an artist's palette his interests merged one into another without a clear-cut division between them. There was no direct path to what he most wanted to do, largely because he had scarcely decided this for himself; and during the 1870s he pursued his original career as a painter, and he also found time to become a family man. Louis married his first wife, Mary

Woodbridge Goddard, on 15 May 1872 and a year later was the father of a daughter, the first of four children (although sadly his first son lived for only three weeks).

Tiffany enjoyed considerable success as a painter during these years, achieving critical acclaim in particular for scenes from his travels in Europe and Africa: the few canvases he sold fetched up to $500 each. He exhibited regularly at the National Academy of Design in New York, where he had been elected an Associate Member. He was a member of the American Watercolor Society and he helped to found the Society of American Artists. He also combined painting with a continuing love of travel, holidaying in Brittany with his family in 1874 and exhibiting an oil painting and two watercolours at the Paris Exposition of 1878.

Opposite: My Family at Somesville, *detail from an oil painting, circa 1888, which shows Tiffany's second wife, Louise, and three of his children walking in the fields with their nurse, while on holiday in the Maine countryside*

Above: *This detail from an Oriental poppy leaded lampshade shows Tiffany's love of vibrant colour*

Despite his success, however, Tiffany was always aware of his shortcomings as a painter: while competent and often brilliant, he felt he could not match the talents of his contemporaries in New York, artists like John La Farge and Edwin Austin Abbey. Tiffany was a perfectionist for whom second-best was not good enough; and he was an extrovert who was frustrated by the limitations of a two-dimensional canvas. These and other factors began to influence his thinking and the final impetus for change came in 1876 at the Philadelphia Centennial Exposition. Tiffany went to this as a painter with nine works on show: he came away as an interior decorator in embryo.

Interior Decoration

Many examples of fine and applied art from England – influenced by the Arts and Crafts Movement and subsequent developments – were displayed at Philadelphia and Tiffany was fascinated by them all. So too was a friend, Mrs Candace Wheeler, whose own considerable artistic talents lay in the fields of needlework and textile design. She was greatly impressed by craftwork from the Royal School of Art Needlework, which had been founded in London to provide profitable work for impoverished gentlewomen; and she determined to do the same in America. With the painter Samuel Colman she formed the Society of Decorative Art in New York, and in 1878 persuaded Tiffany to give classroom lectures on painting and pottery. It was a short-lived association,

totally unsatisfying for Louis, who could see little future in such an amateurish approach to applied art, but it provided the final stimulus he needed: '. . . I have been thinking a great deal about decorative work,' he told Mrs Wheeler in the spring of 1879, 'and I'm going into it as a profession.' Literally within weeks he formed Louis C. Tiffany and Associated Artists with Candace Wheeler and Samuel Colman as partners.

Tiffany was both artist and businessman, but he was also the son of a famous father and that gave the fledgling company immediate access to an untapped, eager and, above all, wealthy market. America was at the height of industrial and commercial prosperity and the nation's new breed of millionaires were eager purchasers of jewellery and other objects at Tiffany & Co., where Louis knew many of them. They wanted homes that reflected the elegance and status of their ornate lifestyles and Louis C. Tiffany and Associated Artists was happy to oblige.

For these 'extravagant people leading extravagant lives' Tiffany and his army of craftsmen and women set about creating extravagant living spaces. Nothing was left out: wallpaper and carpets, fabrics and furniture, light fittings and, most significantly, windows were all coordinated to give a total impression of opulence and elegance. To complete the settings Associated Artists imported rare and costly *objets d'art* and antiques from all over the world (and in the process Tiffany acquired a considerable collection for himself). The result was often a roomful

Above: *The parlour at 8 Fifth Avenue, New York, which Louis C. Tiffany and Associated Artists designed for Mr. J. Taylor Johnston in 1881*

Above: *The dining room at 47 East 34th Street, New York, designed in 1882 by Louis Tiffany for Dr William T. Lusk, who later became his family physician*

22

or even a houseful of expensive, ornamental 'clutter', frequently Oriental or Islamic in origin, for that was what the American *nouveau riche* equated with elegance and status in an industrial age.

The Fifth Avenue home of George Kemp, a rich pharmaceutical merchant, provided Associated Artists with its first commission but others quickly followed. The company was scarcely known to the general public, but inside this small circle of wealth and power it soon reigned supreme. Customers included Mark Twain, Cornelius Vanderbilt II, Lily Langtry (the Jersey Lily), Ogden Goelet and Charles W. Gould; and Tiffany and his artists also designed and decorated interiors for James Gordon Bennett Jr's yacht *Namouna*, then the world's largest private craft, the Madison Square Theatre and the Belasco and Lyceum Theatres, and the Veterans' Room and Library at the Seventh Regiment Armory on Park Avenue, New York.

The White House

The ultimate accolade came in the winter of 1882/3 when Louis C. Tiffany and Associated Artists was invited by President Chester Alan Arthur to redecorate several rooms and a corridor at the White House for a cost of more than $15,000. It was a challenge Tiffany could not resist: he personally supervised the work which was as lavish and ostentatious as any of his designs. The centrepiece was a magnificent floor-to-ceiling opalescent glass screen that replaced one of ground glass as a divider between a first floor corridor and a vestibule. Its many-coloured panels featured American national emblems and it was set off by an equally elaborate ceiling decorated with rosettes; the woodwork was painted crimson and there was a lavish display of palms in gilded pots. What President Arthur thought of this flamboyance is not recorded, although he took a keen interest in Tiffany's designs, inspected each day's work and made suggestions about it. Theodore Roosevelt, who became President in 1902, was seemingly less enthusiastic: two years into his presidency he ordered the screen to be destroyed. It was a costly decision to make: by 1904 Tiffany was at the peak of his glass-making career and a contemporary account put the replacement value of the screen at £50,000.

The opalescent screen was much more than a fixture for a President's house: it was symbolic of yet another change of emphasis in the artistic career of Louis Comfort Tiffany. Just as he had drifted gradually from painting into interior design so he now began to spend more and more time on one particular aspect of decorating. His fascination for glass, planted so many years before and nurtured in the museums and cathedrals of Europe, now flowered into full bloom. The interior decorator bowed out and the glass-maker took centre stage.

Overleaf: The sumptuous drawing room designed in 1881 for Samuel Langhorne Clemens (Mark Twain, the author of The Adventures of Tom Sawyer) *at his mansion in Hartford, Connecticut*

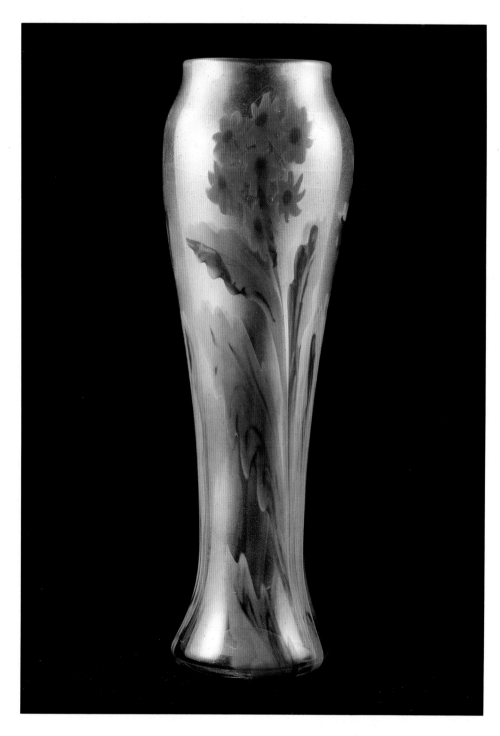

A slender baluster-shaped Paperweight vase made of clear glass

Chapter Two

GLASS-MAKING TECHNIQUES

The Venetians and all the other great glass-makers since the 15th century strove for crystalline transparency and the brilliant effects achieved by skilled etching and engraving, but the Art Nouveau glass-makers broke away from this tradition. Tiffany, in particular, believed in the supremacy of the glass-blower and was somewhat contemptuous of applied decoration. He began to experiment with glass-making techniques as early as 1872 and in 1880 he took out patents for the first of his many innovative forms of glass.

The Tiffany designers and craftsmen produced a scintillating array of highly sophisticated products, but even as we admire them for their intrinsic artistic qualities, it is all too easy to forget the substance from which they are made.

Glass has evolved over many centuries and has long played a vital role in society: it is hard to imagine what we would do without it. Its value for domestic and industrial use is inestimable and despite alternatives like acrylic and plastics, glass is unlikely to be

Above: This Roman purple glass dish was made in the 1st century AD. It was found at Dura in Syria

replaced completely. Its functional value may well diminish but its widespread use in the creative arts will undoubtedly continue, just as it has throughout history. Indeed, glass as a decorative medium almost predates history: glass beads from around 3000 BC have been found in Egypt, and even earlier cultures probably made use of glass formed in volcanic lava.

Essentially glass is melted sand, and as sand in one form or another makes up 60% of the earth's land surface the chance of glass being created naturally, as in volcanic eruptions, is very high. In such circumstances other 'ingredients' also occurring naturally in the earth – minerals such as sodium, magnesium, boron and phosphorus and limestone formed by the fossilized remains of minute living organisms – will inevitably be present. If these fuse with the sand they will affect it chemically, dictating the final properties of the glass once it has cooled – its colour, transparency, reflectivity and so on.

The melting point of glass is between 1300°C and 1550°C but at this temperature the glass is liquid, and to be workable it must be cooled to about 250°C when it takes on a plastic-like consistency. In this state it can be blown, squeezed, twisted, folded or stretched into practically any desired shape; when it cools it can be polished or engraved.

Most civilizations discovered how to make glass but it was not until about 1500 BC that its use became functional rather than decorative. About this time the Egyptians learned how to make glass vessels by the 'core' method, the 'core' being a shaped lump of clay and straw attached to a metal rod and dipped into molten glass. As the glass cooled it was smoothed on a stone slab and handles, feet and decoration could be added before the rod and core were removed.

Right: *A mould blown Roman bottle, dating from the 1st century AD*

The invention of the glass-blower's pipe, often ascribed to the port of Sidon in about 31 BC, was a major advance, for now glass could be shaped into a wide range of useful forms. This simple device is so effective that it has scarcely changed in 2,000 years. It consists of a metal pipe 100–175 cm (39.3–68.8 inches) long and 1 cm ($\frac{1}{2}$ inch) in diameter, with a mouthpiece and heat-resistant wooden grip at one end and a flat, disc-shaped base at the other. The glass-blower collects a 'gather' of mol-

Above: An ornamental bowl and a wine glass made in Venice in the first half of the 16th century

ten glass on to the base and then shapes it by smoothing, swinging, pulling and blowing, or manipulating it with simple tools, reheating the 'gather' if necessary.

For nearly 300 years from the 15th century the Venetians were the supreme glass-makers. They perfected the transparent quality of the material, using a large soda content to produce a glass they called *cristallo* that lent itself well to engraving. Their supremacy was usurped by the Bohemians, who produced a more durable alternative to *cristallo*; and by the English glassmakers around Stourbridge who developed the even stronger lead crystal in the 18th century.

During this time the clarity and crystalline transparency of glassware were the qualities most prized by manufacturers and collectors, while the skill of the glass-cutter eclipsed that of the glass-blower. External decoration was the vogue and the inherent qualities of the glass itself were scarcely considered. Tiffany and other Art Nouveau glass designers changed all that.

Art Nouveau glass-makers revolted against the tradition of crystalline transparency. Instead they sought the lustre effects reminiscent of the iridescence in mother-of-pearl or soap bubbles, effects which were sometimes more akin to metal than glass. To create these effects they used two quite distinct methods. For some, like René Lalique, only the surface of the glass was important: it became a 'canvas' on which to create designs. Their motifs were graphic, moulded in relief or in intaglio, sometimes enhanced by staining or by contrasting clear and opaque areas; but there was no decoration within the glass itself.

Right: *This iridescent Paperweight glass vase is heavily lustred on the outside. It was made in 1919 and stands 66 cm (26 inches) high*

Tiffany had an opposing view. He believed that the beauty in a piece of glass should come from the kiln and he was largely dismissive of decoration applied after it had cooled. He brought the glass-blower back to the centre of the stage after years of playing subsidiary roles to the engraver and the etcher. In essence the aesthetics of Tiffany glass depend on the substance itself, on understanding its intrinsic properties.

There were exceptions and Tiffany's carved glass – where the decoration *was* added after cooling – includes some of the finest pieces he produced. Sometimes the carving was there for purely commercial reasons, simply to hide blemishes in a piece of glassware that would otherwise have been destroyed. But other carved items represent a peak of achievement in this art form: Tiffany employed only the finest engravers, who would often spend many man-hours on individual pieces.

Tiffany began dabbling in rudimentary glass technology as early as 1872. His first attempts at his rented studio in the YMCA building on New York's 23rd Street must have been more like those of a schoolboy with a chemistry set than the expert he became. At any rate there was 'some kind of explosion', members of his family afterwards recalled, and his new wife promptly made him stop. The obsession refused to go away, however, and three years later Tiffany was experimenting at Thill's Glasshouse in Brooklyn where he succeeded in making his first drapery glass (page 56), the forerunner of his many innovations in glass-making.

Above: *Cameo or carved glass is an extremely complicated technique requiring great skill and patience on the part of the glass-maker*

In 1878 Tiffany set up his own glasshouse with a Venetian expert, Andrea Boldini, in charge; but although he learned a good deal from this partnership the enterprise was fated. The works burned down twice, ultimately Boldini resigned and finally the business was wound up.

several years and many experiments later was to form the basis of the famous Tiffany 'Favrile' art glass and ultimately to bring him lasting worldwide renown. It was not a technique invented by Tiffany, but undoubtedly he brought the genre to its highest peak of perfection as an art form.

Nonetheless Tiffany emerged from this experience with considerable knowledge of glass-making techniques and a clear understanding of the direction he wished to take. By October 1880 he was confident enough to apply for patents for three types of glass and these were granted four months later. The first was for glass suitable for tiles and mosaics, the second for window glass and the third for glass with a metallic lustre. This was the iridescent glass that

Above: *Some of these glass plaques may well have been intended for use in decorative windows. Tiffany took out three patent applications in 1880; one for making glass tiles and mosaics; one for plating windows and a third for making glass with a metallic lustre*

Despite the failure of his first glass-making company, Tiffany continued his experiments to improve on the coloured glass that was then available from American manufacturers. This material was being used to produce top-quality articles but Tiffany thought it dull and unattractive . . . literally lack-lustre. He was far more interested in so-called 'imperfect' glass that was being used for everyday objects from wine bottles to preserve jars, where the contents were more important than the containers. 'This glass was richer, finer and had a more beautiful quality in color than any glass I could buy,' he wrote. He realized that this 'beauty' was the result of impurities in the sand used to make the glass, and for several years he and his chemists experimented with ways in which these natural effects could be controlled in the furnace.

Glass was treated with metallic oxides and exposed to acid fumes. It was rolled during manufacture, or two or more pieces were sandwiched or fused together while molten. The results were often unexpected, but gradually by trial and error the experimenters learned how to create the effects that one day would blossom into Tiffany art glass. But at this stage that still lay some way in the future.

Below: *Two iridescent gold vases and an iridescent black and gold vase*

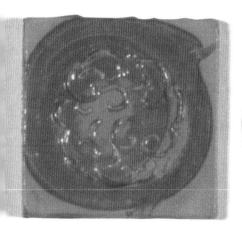

By this time, however, Tiffany was deeply involved with his interior decorating company and this gave him a splendid opportunity to turn theory into practice. His years of experimenting with the chemistry of coloured glass could now be put to practical use and soon he was making decorative glass tiles for the mantles and lighting fixtures that formed part of his interiors. The objects were created under his direct supervision, mostly at the Louis Heidt glasshouse in Brooklyn, and here the many types of glass that later became Tiffany's hallmark began to appear.

Some tiles were transparent and some opaque, while others had an iridescent finish. Smooth marbleized glass with swirling, often accidentally-created shapes beneath the surface contrasted with 'three-dimensional' tiles whose facets caught and reflected light shining on or through them. These irregularities were frequently carefully built into the tiles by use of moulds and took many shapes from the geometric to the abstract.

Above: *Many of Tiffany's interior designs featured lustre and agate tiles. He first used them conventionally in fireplaces, but later went on to incorporate them into table tops and decorative friezes around windows and doorways*

As his confidence increased Tiffany found more adventurous uses for glass, often on a large scale. Now as he recalled his childhood fascination with stained-glass windows and his awe-struck wanderings through the great cathedrals of Europe, Louis C. Tiffany and Associated Artists began to produce magnificently ornate decorated windows for both private customers and public buildings, including churches (see Chapter 3, page 48). As a result the output of glass and the need for further experimentation grew rapidly, and Tiffany became more and more frustrated at having to use a commercial company like Heidt, however excellent they might be. He wanted total control, to use new and untried ideas or revive traditional and well-tried, but often forgotten techniques, as the pieces demanded. He had learned, he told his friend the writer, Charles de Kay, that 'it would be useless to expect to make really beautiful windows unless he could control furnaces of his own where his ideas could be carried out without interference from those who either could not or would not understand.'

Tiffany Glass Company

Not unexpectedly Tiffany's increasingly single-minded preoccupation with glass was a major factor in the break-up of his decorating company in 1882. He himself carried on the original business of interior design as Louis C. Tiffany and Co., while Candace Wheeler and her colleagues became Associated Artists, concerned chiefly with designing and making artistic needlework and wallpaper. 'I think Mr Tiffany was rather glad to get rid of us,' explained Mrs Wheeler, 'His experiments in glass iridescence meant far more to him than association with other interests'. She described the glass rooms where 'Mr Tiffany's experiments in colour went on and where he was working out his problems from bits of old iridescent Roman vases which had lain centuries underground; or finding out the secrets of tints in ancient cathedral windows and the proportions of metals and chemicals which would produce certain shades of colour'.

Few of Louis' friends and business associates were surprised when in 1885 he founded the Tiffany Glass Company 'to provide the manufacture of glass and other materials and the use and adaptation of the same to decorative and other artistic works of all kinds'.

The years of experimenting were drawing to a close and Tiffany stood on the threshold of his career as America's supreme exponent of glass as a decorative medium. With his own glass company and its attendant artists, craftsmen and chemists he could now meet the ever-increasing demand for decorative windows that began to flow into New York from architects throughout America. His true art glass period still lay in the future but most of the methods of making and treating the glass itself had been perfected. That early fascination with ancient glass and the years of

Opposite: *One of Tiffany's later landscape windows dating from circa 1920*

scientific research to emulate it had already produced the wide variety of effects that were to be put to such spectacular use.

Cypriote and Antique Glass

In Cypriote and the similar Antique ware Tiffany set out to capture ancient forms and decoration, seeking the appearance of glass that had been buried for centuries and which had so fascinated him when he came across such objects during his travels. Cypriote has a finely pitted, nacreous surface in imitation of ancient Greek, Roman and Hebraic glass objects whose surfaces had corroded and decayed with time and entombment into myriads of tiny burst bubbles.

Cypriote ware was made by rolling a gather of transparent yellow glass over a marver or rolling table covered with crumbs of the same glass. The crusty surface was heavily lustred but otherwise only minimal, hand-formed decoration was used, the glass relying for its interest and beauty on the irregular, abstract and accidental nature of the production process.

Above: A bulbous Cypriote vase of translucent glass in shades of blues and browns with silvery purple iridescence. The outer casing has an irregular pitted surface, almost like a lunar landscape in miniature
Below: A Cypriote vase of opaque light olive green glass overlaid with dark brown. Around the middle is a pattern of leaves in a gold overlay and the surface of the vase has a purple iridescence

Cameo or Carved Glass

The carving of glass with fine scraping tools and grinding wheels has been practised since ancient times: Tiffany was continuing a tradition started by craftsmen in Alexandria where the art of working glass on a wheel was introduced. With this form of lathe cutting they could produce grooves and facets to create designs in cameo relief or the reverse style of intaglio. Glass carving was greatly in vogue in 19th century England, and in France Emile Gallé used it to produce some of the finest glass of the Art Nouveau period.

Carving to create a cameo effect is a highly-skilled technique. The basis is a vessel formed from two differently coloured glasses, such as opaque white overlying blue, on which the outer white layer is cut, carved and ground away to leave a white design in relief on the blue background. The Portland Vase now in the British Museum, and thought to be of 1st century Roman origin, is the most famous example of this process.

Intaglio cut is simply the opposite: the design itself is cut away from the outer layer leaving motifs in one colour set into the ground of another. As a further alternative Tiffany craftsmen sometimes applied patches of coloured glass to existing objects and carved them in cameo relief.

Above: *This Cameo vase is made from clear glass and has a water lily design overlaid in low relief*
Below: *A Cameo vase made from translucent yellow glass with an outer casing of red glass*

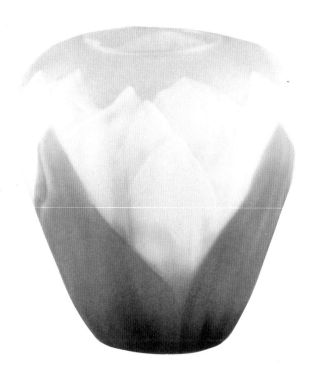

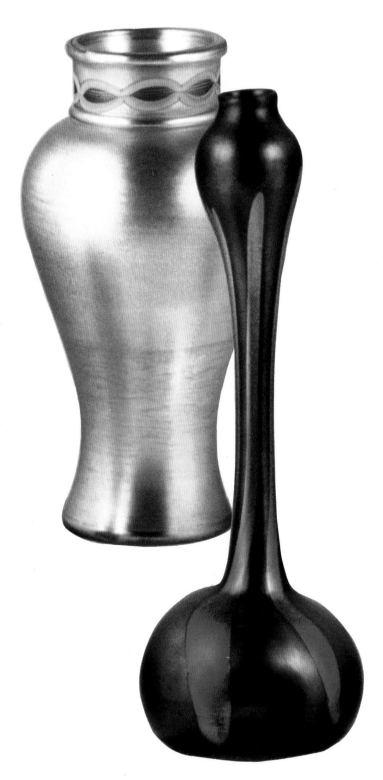

Lustre Ware

When Tiffany filed a patent for lustre ware in 1880 he described the effect as 'a highly-iridescent one and of pleasing metallic luster, changeable from one to the other, depending upon the direction of the visual ray and the brilliancy or dullness of the light falling upon or passing through the glass'.

Tiffany did not claim to have invented iridescence, which involves the use of metallic salts in the glassmaking process. Sir David Brewster (1781–1868), a Scottish physicist, experimented with iridescent effects in 1817. Ludwig Lobmeyer exhibited iridescent glass in Vienna in 1873 and a French company, Monot & Stumpf, showed other examples at the Paris Exposition of 1878. These all had a mirror-like finish, however, unlike the soft, incandescent sheen of the later Art Nouveau pieces.

Lustre ware was made by dissolving salts of rare metals in the molten glass and keeping them in an oxidised state while the glass piece was being made. The object was then subjected to reducing flame which brought the metallic coating to the surface by chemical reaction. Finally the piece was sprayed with chloride which reacted with the metallic surface causing it to crackle into a mass of fine, light-reflecting lines.

Above: An iridescent gold transparent glass vase with Egyptian inspired decoration, which was made in about 1910
Below: An iridescent blue Egyptian onion flower form vase

Different glasses and metals produced different effects, from a dazzling iridescence to a softer, gentler pearl-like sheen, from a rich gold lustre to a deep blue iridescence. The most popular kind of Tiffany iridescent vase was made of blue-green glass with sinuous, silvery plant decorations, while technically speaking the most complicated form of decoration was the peacock feather pattern.

'Jack-in-the-Pulpit' vases were also made in iridescent gold or blue glass. Taking their name from a flower of the convolvulus family, these spectacular and strangely shaped pieces grow from a rounded base into a tall, slender stem which explodes into a huge vertical flower form of undulating glass.

Above: *The Jack-in-the-pulpit vase was one of Tiffany's most popular designs. There are many variations made in all kinds of colour combinations*
Left: *An iridescent gold vase*

41

Lava Glass

As its name suggests, Lava glass was Tiffany's attempt to simulate the effects of volcanic forces on glass: indeed it was originally intended to be called Volcanic glass. It was made by adding basalt or talc to molten glass to produce a black or dark coloured surface with a rough texture, and then covering part of it with gold lustre. The finished articles are in free-form, seemingly accidental styles, sometimes verging on the grotesque. They represent Tiffany's conception of the energy and violence in nature and as such embody early expressionism in glass.

Reactive Glass

Certain kinds of glass are 'sensitive' to heat and change colour in the furnace. Tiffany used this property in a variety of objects (Paperweight vases page 44) where the colour change was part of the production method. In fact the name

'reactive' was given to all glassware that responded to temperature changes even when part of the object was not heat-sensitive. It applies particularly to vessels in which one type of glass is decorated internally with another.

Under this heading come *Rainbow glass*, made from a sensitive, uranium-impregnated material; and *Flashed glass* (or *Pastel Tiffany*), made by coating sensitive glass with non-reactive coloured glass then reheating the resulting object to make it opalescent. In translucent pastel shades or decorative patterns, Flashed glass items became highly popular as tableware, a fact that irritated Tiffany who preferred to think of his products as exclusive rather than commercially successful.

Above: *Three particularly fine pieces of lava glass*
Opposite: *A transparent green glass vase with a peacock feather design*

Paperweight Vases

The rare Paperweight vases by Tiffany were made by encasing a thick layer of decorated glass within a smooth outer layer – in effect trapping the decoration between them. The internal glass or decoration itself gave each piece its descriptive title, so that Red Paperweight has an inner layer of opaque red glass, Reactive Paperweight used an inner layer of reactive glass (which changes colour by chemical reaction when heated) and Millefiori Paperweight incorporated a layer of Millefiori glass.

The Millefiori technique was developed by the Venetians as early as the 2nd century BC. Thin rods of coloured glass were arranged in groups (so that, for instance, five white rods round a yellow rod would produce a daisy) and thinly sliced in cross section. The slices were then incorporated into the vessel.

Supreme examples of Millefiori are the white 'Morning Glory' vases in which the inner vessel is decorated with flowers made of opalescent gold-ruby glass. The first was produced in about 1905 and 50 were exhibited at the 1914 Paris Salon des Artistes Français where Tiffany won his first Honourable Mention.

Above: *All three of these Paperweight vases have a heavy gold iridescent finish on the inside. The one on the right is a perfect example of the scarce Millefiori 'Morning Glory' style. The flowers are in various shades of white with perfectly formed brown stamens*

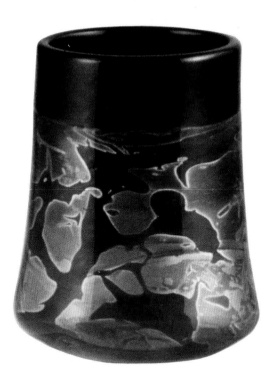

Aquamarine Glass

Derived from the Paperweight style, Aquamarine glass, produced mainly around 1913, was among the most difficult technical feats tackled by the Tiffany craftsmen, and consequently relatively few were made. Their rarity and complexity also made them expensive: even in 1913 pieces sold for up to $250. Aquamarine glass was made by embedding representations of aquatic plants or marine life such as fish, seaweed and sea urchins into an inner layer of glass and enclosing this within an outer layer of green-tinted glass to give the illusion of sea water. This demanded a high degree of glass-making skill as the three ingredients – the marine decoration and the inner and outer vessels – had different fusing points. Aquamarine glass made beautiful but ponderous objects; doorstops, paperweights and fish bowls were produced, besides vases and bowls.

Above: *Left, a Paperweight vase made as an exhibition piece and, right, an Aquamarine vase with a lifelike representation of five goldfish swimming amongst a clump of waterweed*

Agate and Marbleized Glass

Agate ware (sometimes called laminated glass) imitates striated stones such as chalcedony and jasper as well as agate itself. It was made by an ancient technique first used by the Romans in about the 1st century BC and revived by the Venetians in the late 15th-century.

It was produced by putting a number of variously coloured opaque glasses into the same melting pot and heating them together. Sometimes reactive glass was also added to give a laminated effect throughout. Great care had to be taken in the melting process for if the glass became too hot it would fuse into a black mass. When the glass had cooled it was polished or carved to reveal the colours and laminated patterns within.

Sometimes agate glass was plated over plain crystal or coloured glass and design effects obtained by cutting through the agate layer to expose the inner surface.

One variation Tiffany made with Agate ware was Marbleized glass in which he sought to imitate the coloured striations and veinings found in natural marble. Another, called Metallic glass, was conventional Agate ware but in a predominantly reddish-brown colour and heavily lustred both inside and out.

***Above:** An Agate vase, faceted on eight sides, is flanked by two Marbleized glass vases. The two vases on the left were made circa 1910, while the one on the right dates from circa 1915*

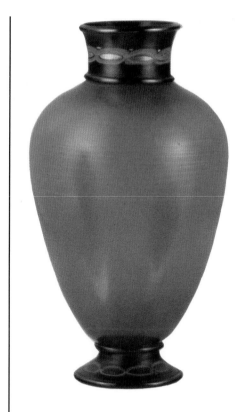

Tel El Amarna

Tel El Amarna vases were inspired by ancient Egyptian vessels from archaeological sites that Tiffany visited in 1878 during his Middle Eastern travels. They take their name from the site of the excavations of Pharoah Akhenaten's capital in Middle Egypt The Egyptians produced glassware for practical purposes with blue being the most popular colour. Tiffany generally used deep turquoise opaque glass to make these large vases, but there are also some in red and ochre as well. They have bold, symmetrical shapes with a matt lustre. Decoration was non-existent or minimal, confined to simple patterns such as palm leaves at base and neck.

The style is sometimes called Egyptian Decorated as well as Tel El Amarna.

Reticulated Glass

Mostly used for lamp bases, candlesticks and inkstands, Reticulated glass was made by blowing coloured glass at high pressure into a cast metal or twisted wire framework so that the glass bulged out through openings in the frame. It is one of the rarest of all Tiffany's forms of art glass and examples are almost impossible to come by.

Above left: *A turquoise blue Tel El Amarna vase. Turquoise blue occurs and again in early Egyptian art*
Above right: *A Reticulated tobacco jar with cover. The framework is made from bands of bronze and the lining is of jade green glass*

Window from the Wayne Community College, Detroit, Michigan

Chapter Three

STAINED-GLASS WINDOWS AND MOSAICS

In the United States during the last quarter of the 19th century stained-glass windows were immensely popular and Louis Tiffany was one of the most celebrated and prolific of designers. Huge demand for his windows meant that Tiffany was less involved with his interior decoration projects, but nonetheless he did find time to make mosaic pictures, designed to be hung on the wall like paintings. He also used the mosaic technique for decorating boxes, mirrors, desk sets and other small items.

Above: The theme for the King Solomon *memorial window comes from I Kings, IX*

Louis Comfort Tiffany was a very talented, creative and enormously energetic man who was not afraid to make radical changes in the direction of his life. During the 1880s he turned from painting to interior design, from decorating to experimenting with glass and ultimately from the theory of glass to its triumphant use in a spectacular series of stained-glass windows and mosaics that brought artistic acclaim on both sides of the Atlantic.

This was no sybaritic son of a wealthy father: certainly he enjoyed the benefits of the Tiffany family's fame and fortune but he was not content to sit back and indulge in a life of indolent luxury. He set his own goals and doggedly pursued them; and on the surface he was a successful, even brilliant entrepreneur. But there was a dark side to this scintillating lifestyle that even wealth, power and talent could not dispel.

Tiffany was a devoted husband and father and the death of his first wife in January 1884 after many years of poor health came as a devastating blow. For a time he seemed to lose the impetus that until then had kept him on a steady, upward artistic path. Painting and interior design, even his beloved glass activities, all became chores and he sought excitement in the theatre. He became a familiar figure on Broadway, a sophisticated man-about-town with chorus girls as his regular companions.

For his friend, the playwright and manager Steele MacKaye, Louis C. Tiffany and Associated Artists had decorated the new Madison Square Theatre several years before. The project was a stunning success with the greatest acclaim going to a magnificent drop curtain. One of the earliest collaborations between Tiffany as a designer and Candace Wheeler and her needlewomen, it was a masterpiece in textiles, a many-hued and lavish, tree-filled landscape that even drew unstinting praise from Oscar Wilde.

Electric Lighting

Now MacKaye planned a new theatre, the Lyceum, and fired with enthusiasm Tiffany offered to decorate it for a percentage of the profits of the first production, a play by MacKaye himself. The Lyceum opened in April 1885 but while the decor was another critical triumph for Tiffany, as an investment it was disastrous. Despite the enthusiastic backing of Oscar Wilde, despite public fascination with the first theatre to be lit entirely by electric lights (with Thomas Edison himself installing the fixtures and footlights) the opening production ran for only two months and Tiffany's profits were non-existent. After years of work he found himself in the financial doldrums. For a time it seemed to make little difference. He continued to patronize the theatre and give 'theatrical' parties that were the talk of New York. Tiffany the artist became Tiffany the showman . . . but not for long.

Charles Tiffany came to the rescue. Appalled by his son's extravagant way of life he suggested they build a new house where all the family could live together, and that Louis would design it. The idea was immediately appealing and Louis threw himself into the project wholeheartedly. The resulting Romanesque mansion on 72nd Street and Madison Avenue, complete with massive arched entrance, balconies and loggias, was an exuberant tribute in stone and wood and, above all, in its interior design to the fact that Louis Comfort Tiffany had lost none of his artistic skills. The English critic and essayist, Edmund Gosse, came to marvel at 'the most beautiful modern domestic building I have ever seen'.

It was a house for a man of substance and fine artistic sensibilities. Naturally there was a studio, but it was no ordinary room: the Tiffany studio was a vast, spacious and lofty top-floor room built round an enormous black chimney that opened into four fireplaces. There was an organ loft and everywhere a scintillating display of lamps, vases and other glass objects of every conceivable colour. Tiffany's private apartment was next to the studio, and downstairs rooms included a ballroom and dining room, both lavishly decorated and in constant use for their owner's social functions.

The house was completed in 1885 and remained Tiffany's town residence for nearly 50 years until his death in 1933 (although his father never in fact lived there). In November 1886 Louis married his second wife, Louise Wakeman Knox, and in due course they raised a second family, including twin daughters. This domestic interlude seemed to have a settling effect on the wayward Tiffany: he virtually turned his back on the theatre and in due course got down to the business he knew best – artistry in glass.

By this time that business was becoming more and more devoted to the creation of stained-glass windows and the related Tiffany mosaics, which were leaded-glass 'pictures' designed for in-terior use. Until then these had been mainly adjuncts to his interior decorating projects, almost by-products, as it were, of larger schemes. Now they became the focus of the creative talents and supreme skills of Tiffany and his craftsmen. Suddenly it seemed that every millionaire and every public company wanted stained-glass work by the Tiffany Glass Company and orders came pouring in from leading architects throughout the United States.

For Tiffany with his fascination for glass it must have seemed like the realization of a long-cherished ambi-

Below: *A firescreen in three panels with a design of white Easter lilies in flower. It was made in about 1910*

tion: but in fact the market for his interior designs was still considerable and he was never able to devote himself exclusively to glass as a pure art form as he might have wished. In 1892, seven years after the formation of the Tiffany Glass Company, he bowed to the inevitable and changed its name to reflect more accurately the work he was doing. The catch-all policy of the Tiffany Glass & Decorating Company was in fact 'the manufacture and sale of glass, decorative objects and materials of all descriptions, and the applying of these materials to buildings and other structures; also the manufacture and sale of furniture, house and church fittings of all kinds, and the conducting of a general decorating business and all things incident thereto'.

It was a range of activities that was to occupy Tiffany not only during the remaining years of the 19th century but well into the 20th century, too, a self-perpetuating business that grew as each successful commission brought in more and more orders for more and more windows or complete decorating schemes.

The Ponce de Leon Hotel at St Augustine, Florida, was a typical example: it was designed by architects Carrère and Hastings for the millionaire Henry M. Flagler as part of his grand scheme to develop Florida as a resort state; and Tiffany's decorating and window work at the hotel led to many orders for similar projects.

Nonetheless it was the stained-glass work that provided most of the work for Tiffany and his growing band of artists and designers, chemists and glass craftsmen. While most of these were American, two Englishmen made an appearance during the stained-glass period, one of them an up-and-coming young designer and the other an established glassblower. Both were to play an important role in the development of Tiffany's business and ultimately, as it turned out, its demise. The first to arrive, in 1890, was Joseph Briggs from Accrington.

Joseph Briggs

In the lists of the world's great centres of culture and the arts the small and far from prepossessing Lancashire town of Accrington would seldom rate a mention. Few people outside Britain have even heard of this small, industrial town, but it now boasts the finest collection of Tiffany glass in Europe, the bequest of Joseph Briggs who went to New York on a three month visit in 1890 when he was 17, joined Tiffany almost immediately and worked with him for more than 40 years.

Information is scant on Briggs' rise to power in the organization but he evidently became Tiffany's personal assistant within a short time while, at the

Overleaf left: The landscape window commissioned by Howard Hinds for his mansion in Euclid Heights, Cleveland, circa 1900. It is now in the Cleveland Museum of Art
Overleaf right: Peace, the Ann Eliza Brainerd Smith landscape memorial window in the First Congregational Church, St Albans, Vermont, circa 1905

·IN·LOVING·MEMORY·OF·
·ANN·ELIZA·BRAINERD·SMITH·

PEACE

NOW·ABID
HOPE·LO
ENDURET
E·GREATE
LOVE·IS

same time, making a particular study of mosaic work. By 1902 he was manager of the Mosiac Department at Tiffany Studios and as such he was involved in some of the most spectacular work carried out by the company in this field.

The explosive growth of stained-glass windows and mosaics was also welcomed by the established glass manufacturers of New York, for the Tiffany Glass Company could not produce the basic raw material in the quantities required. A vast amount of glass, plain and textured, translucent and coloured, opalescent and lustred, was made to Tiffany's strict specifications, and his own craftsmen cut up the pieces and assembled them, usually working alongside the artists who had designed the pieces in question.

Tiffany left nothing to chance. During his years of experimenting he and his colleagues had made a detailed study of mediaeval stained-glass windows, not only of their design and colour but also of their construction. During his travels he had acquired an ancient window and literally taken it to pieces, minutely analyzing every aspect. (One story relates how he was mesmerized by the rich dark colours in this ancient glass until somebody took a cloth to it and showed that the sombre shades were centuries of accumulated dust and dirt.)

Based on his research Tiffany had patented new methods of window construction and this, almost as much as the colour, was responsible for the sheer brilliance and ultimately the enormous popularity of his work. Most of the windows and mosaics made by his competitors started with an outline in leading, with glass fixed into the spaces formed in between. This was too restrictive for Tiffany. He started with the glass: the pieces were cut to match the jigsaw of colours and intricately-detailed shapes of the original designs and the leading 'woven' round them. It was an arduous and time-consuming method that demanded considerable patience and skill but the results were infinitely superior and totally true to his and his artists' designs.

Naturally the raw material in which they all worked was also the subject of intensive investigation – a late 19th century version of research and development. Tiffany's craftsmen and analysts, led by his friend and chief chemist Dr Parker McIlhiney, worked closely with the manufacturers to perfect the various forms of glass required, often with spectacular results.

Through this cooperation, for instance, the Heidt works developed the elegant and impressive material they called 'drapery' glass – an apt description for sheets of coloured glass styled to represent folds in textiles, from the fine pleats of dress material to the voluminous folds of curtains or drapes. To create this attractive and distinctive effect, which gave a three-dimensional look to the finished piece of stained-glass, workmen moved heavy rollers across the face of the molten glass, or literally pushed and pulled it with tongs

Opposite: *The Lauriston Livingstone Stone memorial window in the Third Presbyterian Church, Rochester, New York*

1833　　LAURISTON · LIVINGSTON · STONE　　1920
A · DEVOUT · MEMBER · OF · THIS · PARISH · FOR · THIRTY-ONE · YEARS

wielded in asbestos-gloved hands until the required 'drape' was obtained. It must have been difficult and very hot work.

Despite all this willing effort by the glass factories Tiffany was often frustrated in his attempts to achieve exactly what he and his designers envisaged. In particular the suppliers were not always able to meet Tiffany's colour requirements at a time when colour, to Tiffany, was perhaps the most important feature of the glass. He needed to improve his own glass-making facilities and the solution to that problem involved the second Englishman who was destined to have a significant influence on Tiffany's artistic career.

Arthur J. Nash

Arthur J. Nash was born in Stratford-upon-Avon in 1849 and showed early talents as a glassblower. He was a partner at Webb's Whitehouse Glass Works at Stourbridge, Worcestershire, until Tiffany persuaded him to take his considerable creative abilities and glass-blowing skills to America. For a time Nash experimented with glass for Tiffany but in 1893 the two men went into business as the Stourbridge Glass Company at Corona, Long Island: Tiffany financed the operation and his father also invested a large amount of cash. Parker McIlhiney led a team of chemists while Nash recruited his craftsmen from both sides of the Atlantic. The start of the new enterprise was less than auspicious: soon after it opened the works was burned down, probably by arson, but undaunted the partners built a new factory and set to work.

Naturally the production of glass for stained-glass windows and mosaics formed a large part of the Stourbridge output but significantly a second shop was also opened within the new works to produce blown-glass objects. It was a pointer to a future that for Tiffany was even then only a few years away . . . but meanwhile he was kept busy meeting the demands for interior designs and above all 'pictures in glass'.

From the mid-1880s onwards the range of commissions obtained by Tiffany was enormous. They ranged from the theatrical to the ecclesiastical, from hotels and millionaires' mansions to libraries and chapels of rest. Many of these commissions were for complete decorating schemes but a considerable number involved only the design, construction and installation of windows or mosaics or in some cases both windows and mosaics; and Tiffany took a personal delight in supervizing many of these.

As the years passed this continuing fascination for stained-glass and the everyday demands of his expanding business left him with little enough time for the personal touch in his interior design projects although he was actively involved in some of the larger schemes. One of these was the decoration of the Fifth Avenue home of millionaire Henry O. Havemeyer who insisted on Tiffany's personal attention. The result was yet another triumph for Tiffany and also for

Opposite: The Good Shepherd, *the Crosby Stuart Noyes memorial window, circa 1909*

58

TRVSTEE
1886-1908

CROSBY STVART NOYES
1825   A FRIEND OF BOYS   1908

PRESIDENT
1905 - 1908

Charles A Duncan
December 25th 1858 – July 13th 1924

William G Hegardt
March 27th 1860 – September 22nd

Samuel Colman who came out of semi-retirement to help him.

The Havemeyer house was a stunning blend of the greatest cultures of east and west. Tiffany and Colman created an entirely sympathetic mélange of styles – from Venetian to Viking. Colman invented a method of acid staining to

Above: *The Charles Duncan and William G. Hegardt memorial window at Pilgrim Congregational Church, Duluth, Minnesota, circa 1924*

imitate Japanese lacquer; Mrs Havemeyer told the writer Aline Saarinen, his library ceiling, 'was a sensation!'

In his Newport studio,' she enthused, 'Mr Colman fashioned a mosaic design of multicoloured silks, outlined them with heavy braid and framed panels with carved gold mouldings'.

With praise for this interior still ringing in his ears Tiffany turned to another major project, the design and installation of a memorial window for the new library at Yale University. For this he produced a full-size canvas for his workmen to translate into an opalescent glass window 9.1 metres (30 ft) long by 1.5 metres (5 ft) high containing more than 20 figures. It moved the Boston *Globe* to patriotic fervour: 'No one can stand in this room without a profound feeling of satisfaction that America produces such window works as that of Louis Tiffany. It is a truly wonderful production of this man of thought'.

Equally impressive were later windows for new buildings in Gothic style for the U.S. Military Academy at West Point and for the American Red Cross headquarters in Washington D.C. These and many hundreds more that Tiffany produced to meet an almost insatiable demand for stained-glass across the United States expressed in tangible form his assertion that these were not just windows but works of art, objects to be looked *at* and not merely *through*. It was a small step from there to designing pictures in glass that had nothing to do with windows at all.

Right: *The Frederick A. Wilcoxson memorial window at St John's Episcopal Church, North Adams, Massachusetts, 1910, shows a garden in the Holy Land*

Tiffany mosaics were meant to be hung on walls like paintings.

He had experimented with mosaics in the early days of Louis C. Tiffany and Associated Artists as part of the interior design for the Union League Club on Fifth Avenue which his father had helped to found. By 1889 there was a growing demand for such pieces and around this time Tiffany provided at least five churches in New York and the neighbouring states with interiors that featured mosaics extensively. By the time Joseph Briggs arrived on the scene from England in 1890 Tiffany's Mosaic Department was a major part of the enterprise and it was here that Briggs first made his mark. (It says a great deal for the success of the business around this time that in the four years from 1893 the firm produced as many stained-glass pieces as it had in the previous dozen years or more.)

Mosaic-making

A mosaic is, as a dictionary puts it, 'the fitting together of small pieces (tesserae) of coloured glass'. Civilizations throughout human history have used the techniques to marvellous effect, usually with marble, and Tiffany's mosaics were no exception. Depending on the design his workmen cut out and assembled dozens, hundreds, thousands and in one or two notable works around about a million multicoloured tesserae of iridescent, mother-of-pearl or transparent glass, often backed with gold or metal leaf, with the entire panel bonded together on the reverse with white cement mortar that reflected back light shining on to the surface with a soft, luminous glow. The technique was not only used for major display pieces: tiny mosaics also made up trays, inkwells and the bases for the famous Tiffany lamps that began to appear at this time.

Below: *A sampler of the mosaic design made for the Citizen's Savings Bank, Ohio. This sampler which measures 45 × 90 cms (18 × 36 inches) is in the Haworth Art Gallery, Accrington*

Among the hundreds, possibly even thousands of mosaic 'pictures' created by the Tiffany organization over a period of some 40 years there were several that, even judged against today's world of superlatives, were remarkable in their scope and size. There was the commission for the Catholic cathedral of St Louis, Missouri, for example, in which practically every inch of available wall space was covered with a series of mosaics to designs by the Italian artist Aristide Leonari – totalling around 27.870 sq metres (300,000 sq ft). However, the two projects that perhaps more than any others demonstrate the sheer splendour of Tiffany's work in this field were the colossal glass drop-curtain at the National Theatre in the Palace of Fine Arts in Mexico City and 'The Dream Garden', an extraordinarily beautiful entrance lobby mural for the Curtis Publishing Company in Philadelphia.

The Mexican National Theatre commission was won by Tiffany in 1909, five years after construction work began in this enormous building. The painter and stage designer Harry Stoner produced the 'model', a landscape panorama of the view from the presidential palace with its boundless backdrop of snow-capped peaks, and 20 workmen in the Corona factory spent 15 months faithfully translating it into 167.22 sq metres (1,800 sq ft) of glass containing almost a million tesserae and weighing 27,432 tonnes (27 tons). It astonished the people of New York when it went on show there in April 1911 before being shipped to Mexico City. There it was

built into a finely-engineered construction that took only seconds to raise and lower this astonishing curtain through a system of hydraulic pressure and counterweights.

An immediate result was a call from Edward Bok, editor of *The Ladies Home*

Above: *A turtleback tile and bronze candlestick produced by Tiffany's mosaic department in 1906. Tiffany's candlesticks were not usually sold in pairs*

Journal, who was despairing of finding a mosaic for the Curtis Building, then rapidly nearing completion but 'with no mural for the huge place so insisting on it,' as Bok later explained. Several artists had worked on designs for the piece but the results either remained unfinished or were rejected, and even when Tiffany enthusiastically accepted the commission there was still no original. Finally Bok recalled that the artist Maxfield Parrish had once described a 'dream garden' he would like to build and Parrish readily agreed to paint his 'dream' even if he could not plant it. When completed the resulting mosaic was 14 metres (49 ft) long and 4.6 metres (15 ft) high and over 7,000 people filed past it in awe when it was exhibited in New York before installation.

Tiffany was his usual immodest self when he described the work in a brochure published by Curtis. He even suggested that only glass could have done justice to the artist's 'dream garden': paint on canvas would have been inadequate!

In translating this painting so that its poetical and luminous idealism should find its way even to the comparatively uneducated eye, the medium used is of supreme importance, and it seemed impossible to secure the effect desired on canvas and with paint. In glass, however, selecting the lustrous, the transparent, the opaque and the opalescent, and each with its own texture, a result is secured which does illustrate the mystery, and it tells the story, giving play to imagination, which is the message it seeks to convey.

As a matter of fact, it is practically a new art. Never before has it been possible to give the perspective in mosaics as it is shown in this picture, and the most remarkable and beautiful effect is secured when different lights play upon this completed mosaic.

It will be found that the mountains recede, the trees and foliage stand out distinctly, and, as the light changes, the purple shadows will creep slowly from the base of the mountain to its top; that the canyons and the waterfalls, the thickets and the flowers, all tell their story and interpret Mr Parrish's dream.

I trust it may stand in the years to come for a development in glass-making and its application to art which will give students a feeling that in this year of nineteen hundred and fifteen something worthy has been produced for the benefit of mankind, and that it may serve as an incentive to others to carry even farther the true mission of the mosaic.

Opposite: *The* Minne-ha-ha *window, designed by Mrs Anne Weston and exhibited at the 1893 World's Columbian Exposition in Chicago. This window, which takes its theme from Longfellow's* Hiawatha, *is in the Public Library, Duluth, Minnesota*

Overleaf: The Dream Garden *mosaic in the Marble Lobby of the Curtis Center, Philadelphia*

The many church commissions which Tiffany won during this period must also have given immense satisfaction to this man whose fascination for ecclesiastical windows had helped to mould his early love of glass as an artistic medium. The finished products were not always universally acclaimed. Some found Tiffany's church work too gaudy and ornate, while others deplored his preference for landscapes to more religious themes. Such criticism had little effect on his output, however, for most customers were happy with the results.

Among a great many other projects the Tiffany organization designed and made windows or mosaics for the Wade Memorial Chapel in Cleveland, Ohio; Madison Square Presbyterian Church, St Michael's Church, Middle Collegiate Church and All Angels Episcopal Church, all in New York; the Congregational Church in Petersburgh, Virginia (a Confederate shrine where 15 Tiffany windows were installed); the Peddie Memorial Baptist Church, Newark, New Jersey; and Trinity Church, Lenox, Massachusetts.

For the Russell Sage Memorial Chapel in Far Rockaway, Long Island, the architect Ralph Adams Cram had conceived a grand gothic design and planned to give the stained-glass work to an English artist. He was, however, thwarted by Tiffany who persuaded the chapel's benefactress to 'buy American' instead and promptly produced a landscape window that was one of the biggest he had done at that time, 6.4 metres (21 ft) long 7.62 metres (25 ft) high. Cram had his revenge a few years later in the Affair of the Tiffany Chapel — but to understand *that* we must go to Paris. . .

In 1876 the Philadelphia Centennial Exposition had turned Tiffany from painter to interior decorator. Thirteen years later a major arts exposition in Paris had an equally dramatic effect on his career. First it led to a close and long-lasting artistic and business relationship between Tiffany and Samuel Bing, the French critic and champion of the newly-emerging Art Nouveau style. Secondly it produced commissions that ultimately brought Tiffany wide international recognition; and finally it introduced the American to the art glass vases of Emile Gallé and that was to be the greatest influence of all.

Tiffany's initial emotion at the Paris exposition, however, was one of disconcerted surprise for he found that John La Farge, his greatest rival in the American stained-glass business, had completely upstaged him by displaying a window that everyone was praising as a masterpiece.

The Four Seasons Window
Not to be outdone Tiffany declared that he, too, would create a stained-glass window that Bing could exhibit in Paris. The result was *The Four Seasons*, a stunning, intensely-coloured, intricately-detailed and near-surrealist representation of seasonal flora set against distant landscapes and contained within ornate borders. To a city where the first

Opposite: Summer, *a panel from* The Four Seasons Window

faint stirrings of Art Nouveau were beginning to affect the thoughts and the work of many artists this creation from America was a vast surprise, and its wide critical acclaim brought Tiffany the recognition he felt he deserved.

It also brought a commission from Bing that was equally breathtaking – for Tiffany to produce windows to designs by nine of France's leading artists. It was a major undertaking that tested the Tiffany company's expertise in stained-glass craftsmanship and colour to the utmost, for the artists concerned made no concessions to the practical difficulties of translating their creations from one medium to another.

Paul Ransom produced two designs while one each came from Pierre Bonnard, Eugene Grasset, Henri Ibels, Ker-Xavier Roussel, Paul Serusier, Henri de Toulouse-Lautrec, Edouard Vuillard and Felix Vallotton. After many months of work the ten windows were exhibited first at the annual *Salon du Champs-de-Mars* and later in Bing's *Maison de l'Art Nouveau* when it opened in 1895. The reaction to them was mixed: some felt they lacked the purist approach to art that Art Nouveau supposedly represented, while another school of thought saw them as a triumphant manifestation of both Art Nouveau and the Arts and Crafts Movement, a unique marriage of fine and applied art. Tiffany himself saw them as a vindication both of his own talents and of the supremacy of American stained-glass work, although a leaflet he produced to this effect did not go down too well with his critics. Sadly we cannot judge them for ourselves for these ten windows are now either lost, destroyed or tucked away in private collections.

Columbian Exposition

While this 'canvas-to-glass' experiment was going on Tiffany, again at Bing's prompting, was working on a project that was to be the pinnacle of his ecclesiastical work in the Byzantine style. The Chicago World Fair (the so-called Columbian Exposition) of 1893 was to provide, among other aspects, a showcase for Art Nouveau painters and Tiffany had entered six of his canvases. This was not enough for the admiring Bing who persuaded him to design nothing less than a complete chapel together with two attached display rooms showing the full magnificent range of Tiffany design and craft expertise. It says a great deal for the artist's standing at the time that the World Fair organizers quickly made room and lighting facilities for this major exhibit even though no provision had originally been made for stained-glass work. It helped, of course, that the Fair's director and coordinator of painted decorations was a former Tiffany artist Frank D. Millet, while Candace Wheeler was also a leading display organizer.

The inclusion of the chapel and display rooms might have been a last-minute decision but, as it turned out, it was the correct one: contemporary reports showed that they attracted more attention from visitors than any other display of American industrial art. They also won 54 medals at the Fair (but history doesn't record whether Tiffany

was delighted or disappointed that his father's company won 56.) All this must have pleased him immensely since he had described his company's exhibit, rather grandiloquently, as 'the introduction of new and original ideas . . . equal in merit with the best that has been done'. But then Tiffany was not given to modesty.

Above: The lectern, altar and font from the World's Columbian Exposition Chapel showing the peacock reredos in the background. The peacock is a symbol of immortality

71

The chapel was a masterpiece of style and form, elegantly simple in design concept with steps leading to an altar below a series of concentric, columned arches that in turn framed a reredos; and for illumination there were a dozen stained-glass windows and an elaborate sanctuary lamp suspended from the domed ceiling. That was the 'canvas', the outline on which Tiffany set to work and he filled it with breathtaking Byzantine artistry, with scintillating colours from almost a million pieces of mosaic glass. Each item was stunning in its individual treatment yet each contributed to the opulent, almost ostentatious whole.

The altar was in stark white marble with a mosaic frontal in white and iridescent glass. The soaring ciborium that arched above featured a geometric relief pattern tinged with gold while the supporting pillars were randomly decorated in contrasting reds, greens and browns. Inlaid mosaic inscriptions on religious themes were set into the steps while the tabernacle over the altar was in richly jewelled filigree. The visual highlight of the chapel was the magnificent reredos which contained some of the most complex mosaic work that Tiffany and his craftsmen ever conceived and executed, a brilliant pictorial representation of peacocks and scrolls of vine leaves in blue and green iridescent glass set into black marble.

Before its triumphant appearance in Chicago Tiffany's chapel was first shown in New York and after the World's Fair it returned once more to New York. It was purchased by a wealthy widow, Mrs Celia Whipple Wallace, and donated to the Cathedral of St John the Divine in New York City where – after three years languishing in Tiffany's own studios – it was eventually installed in the crypt and used for all services until 1911.

Left: A close-up view of the lectern and altar in the World's Columbian Exposition Chapel
Opposite: Pumpkins and Beets, a window in the Impressionist style

Unwittingly it then gave Ralph Adams Cram an opportunity to get his own back on Tiffany for 'stealing' the stained-glass window contract for the Russell Sage Memorial Chapel. St John's Cathedral had been built in romanesque style and the chapel was a perfect match. But in 1911 Cram's architectural firm redesigned it on gothic lines and sealed off Tiffany's ecclesiastical masterpiece. It was a hollow victory: five years later Tiffany repossessed his chapel and moved it to Laurelton Hall, his sumptuous mansion on Long Island, where he consecrated it as 'a temple of art, not a place of worship'.

Complementing the chapel at the Chicago Exposition were Tiffany's self-styled 'dark room', in varying shades of green, and his 'light room' where silver and opal were the dominant colours. Again there were richly ornate stained glass windows and mosaics to set off the decor . . . but even more significant were a variety of fixtures using iridescent glass. By 1893 Tiffany had been experimenting with glass for almost two decades; he had spent four years reflecting on the art glass of Emile Gallé that he had seen in Paris; and he had installed Arthur J. Nash at the Corona Glass Factory where a workshop for blown-glass objects was an essential feature.

A leaded lampshade in the Landscape design, circa 1907

74

Chapter Four

LAMPS AND LIGHTING

To many people the name Tiffany is synonymous with lamps and they are undoubtedly one of the most outstanding examples of his art. The Tiffany Studios Lamp Shop came into being in the 1890s — originally to make use of the offcuts from the stained-glass and mosaic workshops — and over the years it produced many hundreds of designs for lampshades and lamp bases for use with candles, oil and the new electric light bulbs. The 1890s and the early 20th century were great years for Tiffany; he was now world famous, the leading American exponent of the Art Nouveau style, and winning both international honours and huge commercial success.

When thousands and thousands of sheets of coloured glass are cut up into millions of small and intricate shapes there are bound to be huge quantities of little pieces left over. So it was in the Tiffany stained-glass and mosaic shops. It seems fanciful to suppose that the first of the world-famous Tiffany leaded lamps was put together from some of these scrap pieces of coloured glass left lying on the workshop floor, but that is very probably what did happen, although not by accident but by careful planning and design. In hindsight this development was almost inevitable.

So too was the emergence in the early 1890s of Tiffany's blown-glass lamps. Once Arthur Nash and his craftsmen colleagues started producing the Tiffany-inspired vases and bowls that were to become the ultimate expression of American art glass it was natural that they should use their glassblowers' pipes and their glassblowing skills to fashion lampshades. Blown-glass shades actually pre-dated the leaded-glass varieties by a year or two although it was the latter that had the greatest mass-appeal.

It was not as simple as that, of course: all these lamps did not spring into being overnight, as it were, at Tiffany's whim. They were the outcome both of a variety of artistic influences, some rooted in his own early childhood, others dating from his travels in Europe and the Middle East, and of outside commercial factors such as the invention of the electric light bulb and Tiffany's desire to mass-produce high-quality glassware for the widest possible market.

For most of his life he had been devoted to the study of glass, not only with the substance itself and its colours and textures, but also with the play of light on and through its surfaces, with the infinite possibilities of transparent and opaque glass, with the opalescent and the iridescent. His fascination for stained-glass windows and with forms of ancient earth-entombed glassware had not merely satisfied a student's curiosity but had completely shaped his life.

Love of Colour

Lighting had played an essential role in Tiffany's interior decorating schemes but in the early days it was a subordinate role to other, more demanding aspects of these complex projects, such as furniture and windows. Nonetheless, given his love of colour, his passion for glass and his intense interest in light and illumination there is little wonder that he eventually produced lamps for his customers. The wonder is that he didn't venture into lamp production as a major enterprise earlier than he did.

Tiffany, of course, may have been dissatisfied with hitherto available sources of artificial gas and electric light. Even though electric power had been introduced several years before, gas was still the chief means of lighting domestic and public places at this time and many homes continued to use oil-lamps or even candles. In fact Tiffany had used gas light-fixtures in his lavish decoration schemes for the White House and for several millionaires' mansions and had designed a variety of lamps for use with candles or with bases to hold paraffin. But it was the advent of electric lighting that spurred him to begin the production of lamps in quantity and within a few years they were to represent by far the biggest output of his studios.

Thomas Edison

The lighting revolution began in 1879 when Thomas Edison perfected his carbon-filament incandescent light bulb. Tiffany was quick to see the benefits of this new form of illumination, not only on a utilitarian but also an *artistic* level and he was doubtless delighted to work alongside Edison on the Lyceum Theatre project some years later. The result was highly acclaimed. In an effusive outpouring the New York *Morning Journal* reported, 'Everything was a departure from the hackneyed forms of theatrical decoration. The electric light from the clustered globes pendant from the ceiling is soft and pleasantly diffused. Similar lights smoulder under the sconces along the face of the gallery, like fire in monster emeralds . . . But these things are not obtrusive. A master hand has blent them into a general effect, avoiding all aggressive detail'.

For projects such as the Lyceum, Tiffany had relied on a number of commercial glassworks to produce pieces to his designs, but with the opening of the Corona factory in 1893 he was, at long last, able to control both experimentation and production. Tiffany was a fair but firm taskmaster with his own sometimes highly idiosyncratic ideas about what could and could

Above: *A turtleback tile and favrile glass chandelier, circa 1905. Turtleback tiles have an uneven surface which reflects and refracts light in a most attractive and decorative manner*

not be achieved, a perfectionist who would often insist that his long-suffering workmen carried out so-called 'finished' projects over and over again until he was satisfied.

The time and cost of all this effort was of no account to Tiffany. While Arthur Nash and his fellow glass-makers believed that they knew the limitations of their craft, Tiffany had no such mental barriers to creativity. 'What is thinkable is do-able', he would declare; and it sometimes took thousands of dollars and literally years of work to demonstrate that some of his more outrageous ideas were not 'do-able'. As a business, in fact, the glassworks never made a profit but the loss was more than offset by the success of his other enterprises.

Despite these costly failures Tiffany's extravagant demands often did prove eminently 'do-able' and at the Corona works the seeds of his many years of research and study, of design and experimentation, now began to flower into the fantastic forms of glass that were soon to astound all who saw them, from artists and art critics to glassmakers and collectors, and from millionaires to the man in the street. In a vast outpouring of technological innovation the works began to produce blown-glass objects with iridescent and lustre effects, Cypriote ware that recreated the pitted and corroded surfaces of ancient, entombed glass, Lava glass that copied the effects of natural forces on the material, Agate or Laminated ware with its multicoloured striations.

Opposite: A Fireball table lamp

'Favrile'

In November 1894 Tiffany registered the trademark 'Favrile' at the U.S. Patent Office to describe his blown glass. Now perhaps the most famous word in the art glass field it was accurately if somewhat prosaically patented as 'a composition of various coloured glasses, worked together while hot'. There is strong evidence to suggest that when Tiffany was looking for a collective word for his new glassware Arthur Nash proposed 'fabrile' from the Old English meaning 'handmade' or 'belonging to a craftsman or his craft'. For a time pieces were labelled with this mark but it was quickly changed to 'Favrile', explained in an 1896 brochure as 'a material produced by what is believed to be a new formula, the outcome of a number of experiments instituted by and carried on by Mr Louis C. Tiffany'.

Although the Corona factory produced its first art glass in 1894, another two years passed before Tiffany felt ready to launch his new products on the open market. From this one might suppose he was uncertain of their commercial appeal, but it is more likely that he realized that the market for such innovative products had first to be created.

He seemed to have no such doubts about the *artistic* appeal of his products, however, and most of the first year's output from Corona was sent to a number of leading museums and art

Above: One of several versions of the Favrile mark

galleries in America, Europe and the Orient. These ranged from the Smithsonian Institute in Washington D.C. to the Louvre in Paris, from the Imperial Museum of Fine Art in Tokyo to the Metropolitan Museum of Art in New York which received 56 items as a gift from Henry Havemeyer, probably the first *bona fide* collector of Tiffany art glass.

In later years some museums denied that their collections had been donated by Tiffany or his friends during this period, but nonetheless many institutions undoubtedly did receive such gifts. Whether the donations came from Tiffany the benefactor or Tiffany the highly-skilled publicist is open to debate; but they had the desired effect of introducing his art glass to a wide and discerning audience and preparing the way for the commercial launch two years later.

When that day came it was largely Tiffany's vases and bowls that were singled out for artistic appraisal. He was acclaimed widely as the American Art Nouveau exponent *par excellence*. The blown-glass lamps that formed part of this first 'Favrile' collection made comparatively little impact on the arts world at the time; but in due course the public, in particular, began to clamour for them, and the appearance of leaded lamps a few years later created Tiffany's first mass market. It is probably true to say that while the original inspiration for vases and bowls came from the European and Oriental sources the lamps were an American phenomenon. Factors that influenced their inception

are nonetheless apparent.

Edison's incandescent bulbs had been used to back-light the stained-glass windows of the Tiffany chapel at the Chicago World's Fair; and here also were two more of the seemingly unconnected factors that could well have influenced Tiffany when he started to think about his lamps. Among the features of the chapel was an elegantly beautiful baptismal font with a dome-shaped cover made from more than a thousand pieces of coloured glass fixed into leading. The sanctuary lamp or electrolier (chandelier) hanging from the ceiling was composed of 'turtle-backs', turtle shell-shaped glass panels, lit by bulbs. Significantly some of the earliest Tiffany lamps combined electric lighting with dome-shaped stained-glass shades.

The English Arts and Crafts Movement had been an important influence on Tiffany, dating from his early years as a painter. This aesthetic revolution inspired by William Morris and his followers had attracted him during his first youthful ventures into Europe. He was immediately in sympathy with their naturalistic approach to art, their aim of reviving individual craftsmanship which had been swamped by 19th century industrialization and their desire to take the appreciation of art to the widest possible audience, to make art and artistic objects available to everyone and not just the wealthy and privileged few.

To do this the Movement's advocates saw much of their role as freeing the craftsman from slavery to machinery, from factory labour, and restoring him to the 'simple life' that technology had usurped. Suiting action to words Morris and several friends had founded a craftsmen's collective in 1861, a company to undertake decorative and artistic commissions: it was ultimately successful and its influence is still felt to this day.

Tiffany found this idea appealing too. He had been brought up to appreciate the satisfying collaboration of artist and artisan in his father's workshops and he was later to run his own businesses on much the same lines. In this way he could rightly be regarded as the leading exponent of what became an American variation of the Arts and Crafts Movement, even if he coupled all this with an innate American flair for invention and innovation and an entrepreneurial approach to business that was often pure showmanship.

Wide Appeal

But in one significant way Tiffany departed from the Arts and Crafts ideals. To Morris machine technology was anathema: to Tiffany it was a way of making his products available to the widest possible audience and he was never afraid to use machinery if this was the most efficient means of manufacture. The painting of pictures, the devising of interior decoration schemes, the production of windows and mosaics and, in particular, the making of his 'Favrile' vases and bowls, were all individually crafted objects and settings that were true to Morris's beliefs. Each work was a unique personal expression of Tiffany's artistic

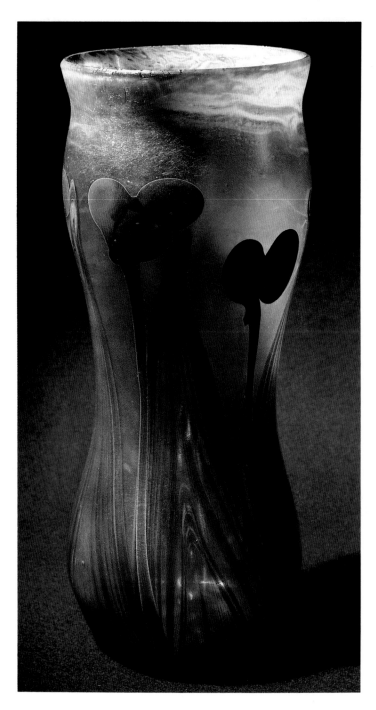

Above: *A favrile vase made in 1896. As with all Art Nouveau artists, the influence of nature and natural forms is very evident in Tiffany's work*

creed. In a general sense the same holds true for his lamps, which first appeared about 1895 and grew rapidly in popularity as Edison's electric light bulb became widely available. For the first time in his career Tiffany was producing objects that were not only fashionably artistic but also eminently useful. They had a mass appeal that he probably underestimated at the beginning. So great did the demand become, particularly for the leaded lamps which were introduced in 1899, that he was forced to abandon individualism and adopt mass-production techniques: within a year or two there was a virtual assembly-line at the Corona works to put leaded lampshades together.

The prototype of a leaded shade followed Tiffany's overriding principle of cutting the glass pieces to conform with the artist's design and 'weaving' the leading round the glass; and in this way it was no different from an original stained-glass window or a mosaic. But from this prototype could then come copies of the leading, together with the copper templates of the glass pieces, so that both could be produced and assembled in quantity, often in a range of sizes. In this way hundreds and sometimes thousands of samples of each pattern were made, and most of them sold as quickly as they were put on to the market. Imitators soon appeared on the scene to cash in on the trend but none ever matched Tiffany for quality. Most of these competitors are now long-forgotten and even surviving examples of their products are usually called 'Tiffany lamps' whatever the origin.

Tiffany's artists produced a constant flow of new designs, literally hundreds of them, and while he himself contributed only a few of these, it is easy to see in looking at them, that his creative influence was present in every one. He also deliberately built individuality into his mass-production system, giving the mainly female assembly-line artisans, who fashioned the shades, the freedom to choose their own colours and textures from the wide Corona range. (By the end of the century that range really was phenomenally large: an inventory in 1898 showed a stock of between 200 and 300 tons of glass in as many as 5,000 colours and varieties.)

Leaded Lamps

The result was a series of leaded lamps in which quantity was combined with quality, so that while the outline of a piece might be identical to many others, its intrinsic character was entirely unique. The Dragonfly and the Wisteria, two of Tiffany's most popular leaded lamps, are prime examples. Coincidentally they were both designed by women, two of many who were encouraged by Tiffany to take an active role in his business at a time when the Suffragette Movement had scarcely begun and votes for women on either side of the Atlantic were still many years away.

Opposite: *A miniature Wisteria lampshade with a bronze Tree trunk base. The standard Wisteria lampshade is made up of more than a thousand pieces of painstakingly selected glass*

The Dragonfly is an elegant interpretation of Art Nouveau in its finest form, in which the spread-winged insects hang head-down to form the fringe of the dome-shaped lampshade. Each wing is made up of literally scores of minute fragments of coloured glass set into intricately-formed leading, while the rest of the shade is a random assembly of larger tesserae, often highlighted with semi-precious stones. For the women in the production line the design allowed for practically unlimited variations on the original theme, so that while one lamp could have red-eyed insects with iridescent wings another might feature green eyes and yellow wings.

The Wisteria lamp, which in 1902 won an award at the International Exhibition of Modern Decorative Arts in Turin, was the work of Mrs Curtis Freschel, another of the highly-paid women designers at the Tiffany studios. Again, the multi-tesserae intricacy of its random-edged shade depicting Wisteria blossom, set over a bronze stem base fashioned to represent the tree trunk, lent itself to many colour variations from deep blue to an almost silvery hue. From the Wisteria also sprang a whole line of floral shades, including Laburnum, Grape and Apple Blossom.

Clara Driscoll went to work for Tiffany in 1887, trained as a designer and ultimately became one of his finest artists and the head of the design department. By 1904 she was also one of the highest-paid women in America — which probably means in the world — earning over $10,000 a year. Mrs Driscoll was responsible for many of Tiffany's classic leaded lampshade patterns, from flora and fauna to geometric and abstract, and the climax of a distinguished career came in 1900 when her Dragonfly design won a prize at the Paris International Exposition. The Rose and Butterfly lamps are also her designs.

***Above:** A Dragonfly table lamp, designed by Mrs Clara Driscoll, on a bronze Twisted vine base. The pendant was designed to hang on one of two hooks inside the shade*
***Opposite:** The Grape table lamp, designed by Mrs Curtis Freschel*

Another lamp brought a major triumph for the Tiffany company at the Turin Exhibition, where it won the Grand Prix. This was the famous Lily Pond design, usually attributed to Tiffany himself, a gorgeous cluster of morning-glory shades on 18 slim bronze stems springing from a bronze base in the shape of a lily-pad. This later formed the model for a wide range of table and standard lamps in green or gilt bronze, with as few as three or as many as 20 shades.

Artistry in the shades was matched by artistry in the bases of the Tiffany lamps, for he saw them as complete objects of the finest beauty. With the opening of a foundry and metal shop at the Corona factory in 1897, bronze and copper bases as well as glass shades could be made on the premises and many of them reached a high level of artistic excellence. For this famous Nautilus lamp, an early model introduced in 1899, the range of variations included one with a bronze mermaid base designed by the sculptor Louis A. Gudebrod, holding up a genuine nautilus shell containing the light-fitting and the bulb. Other versions had simpler bases but with leaded-glass shades faithfully copying the convoluted nautilus shape.

As the 20th century dawned Tiffany was in his fifty-second year and approaching the peak of his cultural and

commercial success. Artistically he was world famous, fully accepted as a major contributor to the flourishing style of Art Nouveau that had become the darling of the arts cognoscenti. His art glass was now highly acclaimed and widely imitated – but rarely matched in either quality or style – and as the years passed, there came more and more tangible evidence in the shape of medals and other prestigious awards from leading exhibitions in both the old world and the new.

Opposite: *The Lily lamp, designed by Mrs Curtis Freschel, came in combinations of 3–24 units, but 3, 10, 12 and 18 were the most popular*
Above: *A Nautilus table lamp*

In 1900 the Tiffanys, both *pére et fils*, were honoured at the enormous *Exposition Universelle* in Paris, which was dominated by Art Nouveau, then at its zenith. Many countries mounted national exhibitions and a large section of the United States Pavilion was devoted to the work of Tiffany and Co, and Louis Tiffany. The US Pavilion also showed the very first escalator. It probably raised few eyebrows for the world had witnessed a whole spate of scientific wonders in the previous decade, beginning with M. Eiffel's amazing tower and including photographic film, international telephone calls and wireless telegraphy, safety razors and air-conditioning, and in France itself the discovery of radio-activity by Becquerel and radium by the Curies and the world's first public film show, following the invention of the motion picture.

Showered with Honours

The exhibition was a personal triumph for Charles Tiffany: by then 88 and a sick man, he was doubtless cheered when the Paris judges awarded Tiffany and Co. three Grand Prix, ten gold, ten silver and two bronze medals. Clara Driscoll's Dragonfly lamp (page 84) also won a prize here, while Louis Tiffany himself not only won a gold medal but was created a knight (chevalier) of the French Legion of Honour; and, so too, was Charles T. Cook who had succeeded Charles Tiffany as president of the jewellery company.

As the new century progressed more honours came Louis' way . . . at the St Petersburg, Pennsylvania, Exhibition;

at the Buffalo Pan-American Exposition in 1901; at the Turin Decorative Arts Exhibition in 1902; the Louisiana Purchase Exposition in St Louis (1904); the Jamestown Tri-Centennial (1907); the Seattle Exhibition (1909); the Paris *Salon des Artistes Français* (1914) and at the Panama–Pacific Exposition in San Francisco, held to celebrate the opening of the Panama Canal in 1915.

Those were the artistic achievements; the commercial rewards came in the form of ever-rising sales of Tiffany art glass, as the vases and lamps and,

subsequently, a vast range of other items from the decorative to the useful emptied the pockets and filled the homes of growing numbers of people.

Tiffany's method of selling was as idiosyncratic as his production techniques. In a sense he was manufacturer, wholesaler and retailer combined, for the glass was never sold to shops and stores but simply placed with them on a sale or return basis – at prices firmly laid down by Tiffany himself. Every piece remained his property until it was sold, when the retailer passed the proceeds, less his commission, back to Corona. If an item was unsold after three months it was returned to the factory; and if it still failed to sell after passing through three retailers' hands, Tiffany would either give it to a friend, sell it at a discount to an employee or simply order it to be destroyed. Since the selling prices were high (a large lamp could be as much as $750, a small fortune in the early 1900s) this was probably the fate of many exceptional pieces.

Thousands of items did sell, of course, and the Corona factory expanded to meet the demand: before long the original two shops had grown to at least seven. In September 1902 the factory also changed its name, from the Stourbridge Glass Company to Tiffany Furnaces; and by this time, too, the Tiffany Glass and Decorating Company had become, simply, Tiffany Studios.

At the Corona works Arthur J. Nash was now being assisted as manager by two of his sons, Douglas and Leslie, while Dr Parker McIlhiney's team of chemists had also grown in number.

Above: *A miniature Apple Blossom table lamp on a Tree trunk base. The Apple Blossom design was developed from the very popular Wisteria shade designed by Mrs Curtis Freschel*
Opposite: *A Dragonfly and Waterflowers lamp on a base set with four turtleback tiles. This is one of the rarest lamp bases of all*

89

One particularly important shop was devoted to experimental work on new methods and designs. It was headed by Tom Mandeville, an expert glassblower who had helped Tiffany to develop his iridescent and lustring techniques. But while both he and the Nashes were extremely gifted glassmakers, craftsmen undeniably as good as any in the world, they were not the originators of ideas but the followers of Tiffany's artistic direction. It was his insistence, often to the exasperation of his more practical employees, that turned the 'thinkable' into the 'do-able'.

Immense Creativity

Tiffany had the imagination, unrestricted by technical know-how, to see beyond the possible; flaws in the glass, that other manufacturers sought to avoid, became part of the artistic creation and often he would turn accidents in the workshops into new forms of glass. But he was not a rigid dictator: he encouraged his workers to experiment for themselves and let them handle priceless and irreplaceable pieces from his own collection of ancient glassware so that they could copy the effects.

While Tiffany Furnaces was devoted largely to the production of glass and glass objects Tiffany Studios, after 1900, began to expand in several directions, not all of them commercially successful. Interior design commissions were still being undertaken, though to a lesser extent than before, and to this business Tiffany now added departments concerned with making or obtaining a heterogeneous collection of household

Above: After his father, Charles Lewis Tiffany, died in 1902, Louis Tiffany moved all his glass-making departments to what was to become Tiffany Studios, on the corner of Madison Avenue and 45 Street. The building was sold in 1918, soon after the inauguration of the Louis C. Tiffany Foundation

objects and decorating materials of all kinds from wood and metal fittings to carpets, rugs and other fabrics.

Under his trademark the company supplied cigarette boxes and lighters, inkstands and jardinières, clocks and thermometers, pin-cushions and salt cellars, punch-bowls and photograph frames, trinket-boxes and desk-sets, letter-openers and finger bowls, and dozens of other items in all kinds of styles and materials, including jewelled and enamelled ones.

Enamelware was a growing business in itself by the early 1900s. A small unit with limited facilities had been set up by Tiffany in 1898, under the direction of Julia Munson and the artist Patty Gay. In 1903 it was enlarged to tackle a wide range of vitreous enamel work, by which ground glass was applied to metal objects and fired in the furnace until the glass fused to the metal, often with the

Left: A large sterling silver platter from Tiffany Studios
Right: A circular enamelled copper plaque, 30 cms (12 inches) in diameter, with a floral decoration

famous Tiffany iridescent effect. The metal objects themselves – usually in copper, brass or bronze, but sometimes gold or silver plated – were made in the Corona foundry and included an enormous variety of items from small boxes and lamp bases to elevator doors.

Favrile Pottery

Today examples of Tiffany enamelling are rare; and so too is Favrile pottery, for this was another venture that lasted for only a short time. Possibly it seemed a natural extension of glassware at the time, but the potters found it difficult to create items from clay that could match the beauty of glass, and to coat them with iridescence as Tiffany demanded, and the examples that survive appear cumbersome by comparison.

Moulded or thrown, the ceramic lamps or vases were largely coloured green, brown, blue or unglazed white, with various designs including copies of ancient bronze artefacts and American Indian pottery, often decorated with floral or marine motifs. Favrile pottery was introduced at the St Louis Exhibition in 1904 but it was never strongly promoted and did not sell in any quantity.

In February 1902 Charles Tiffany died aged 90 and his son became vice-president and artistic director of the family jewellery company. But this time Louis was also making jewellery: it had begun as a development of the enamelling department, but gradually enamelled jewellery gave way to traditional methods, using gold, silver and other materials set with precious and semi-precious stones and Favrile glass. In 1903 an artistic jewellery department

Right: A ceramic vase with a raised pattern of milkweed stems and pods. 25 cms (10 inches). Tiffany's favrile pottery is much rarer than his glass

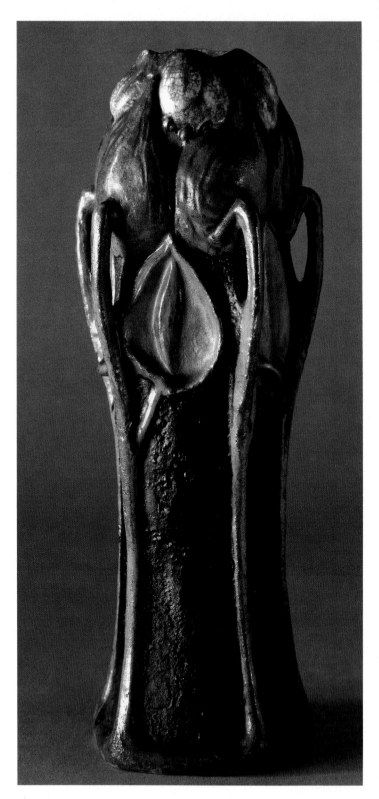

Above: Another ceramic vase with a design based on natural forms; this time a stick of celery provided the inspiration

was opened at the Tiffany and Co. showrooms on Fifth Avenue, and Julia Munson moved from the enamelling department to take charge of it. The department sold items made both by Tiffany Studios and Tiffany and Co. but as they were all marked 'Tiffany and Co.' precise identification is sometimes difficult.

Jewellery

Many pieces do bear the unmistakable hallmarks of Louis Comfort Tiffany, however, in their bold yet sensuous Art Nouveau styling and in a painter's natural use of colour, from fiery red to pale opal. Following Tiffany's rough sketches, or taking inspiration from his huge collection of Oriental and Middle Eastern art objects, his craftsmen made a wide range of jewellery from brooches, girdles and dress-clusters to necklaces, hatpins and tiaras.

They were greatly admired: one necklace and matching girdle moved *The Craftsman* magazine to declare:

The necklace suggests the metal work of the Etruscans but in this piece a new art has lent a charm unknown in the old world. The translucence of the green and blue enamel upon silver, the deep color quality of the sapphires, the sheen of the garnets set at the center of the flower forms, combine to gratify the eye as the intense, unrelieved yellow of the Etruscan gold could never do. The girdle uses as its motif the bitter-sweet. Its boldness counterfeits the hand of Lalique himself, while its

delicacy makes it suitable for personal adornment and use rather than as a museum piece. It is a masterpiece of American craftsmanship and at the same time an artistic creation of great value.

Admiration does not always equate with sales, however, and the jewellery venture was a financial failure: too much time and effort was spent on most of the pieces which were very expensive as a result. Tiffany Studios ceased to manufacture them in about 1916, although the department itself remained open at Tiffany and Co. until 1933.

For Tiffany in the first decade of the new century these were minor setbacks, imperceptible pauses in his upward progress to international fame and personal triumph. He was the head of a large and expanding, commercially successful and artistically satisfying business empire with the respect and admiration of more than a hundred highly-skilled employees. He was a happily married man with a growing family of children and grandchildren and a country estate on Long Island as well as his town house. He loved playing host at lavish parties or being entertained; and if his second wife with her somewhat puritanical upbringing was less than enthusiastic about his social life it was a view that saddened rather than deterred him.

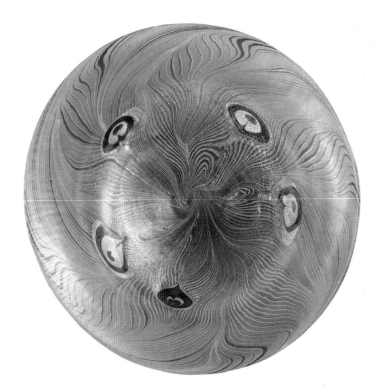

Tiffany had crowned a long association with Yale University by providing one of his finest decoration schemes to mark their bicentennial in 1901. The awarding of an honorary Master of Arts degree by the university two years later was as deeply satisfying as any of the major awards he had won at exhibitions, for he had often regretted his early lack of a college education.

But if Tiffany refused to see any clouds on his horizon, the clouds were there nevertheless. The world was trembling towards the brink of the Great War and that was to change not only its political direction but its artistic direction, too.

Opposite: *Peacock necklace designed by Louis Tiffany. The medallion depicts a peacock in a mosaic of opals, amethysts and sapphires*

Above: *This large favrile glass plate with its swirling design represents the epitome of Art Nouveau design*

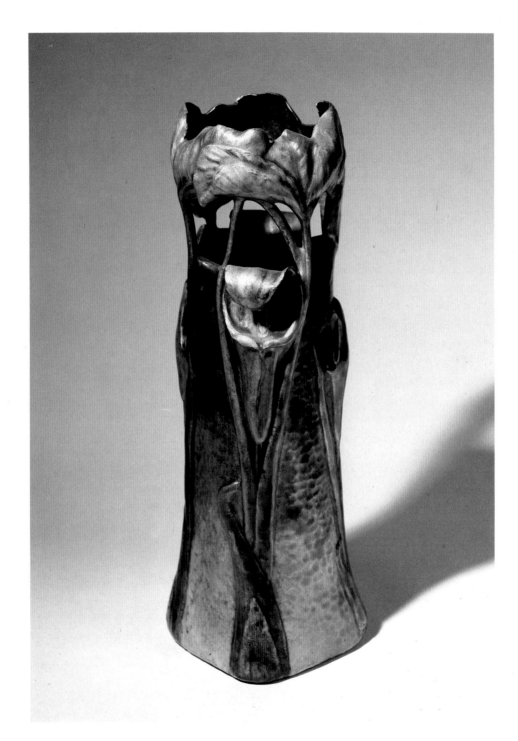

An enamel on copper vase with openwork decoration

Chapter Five

THE FINAL YEARS

At the beginning of the 20th century no art-loving household in the United States was complete without a Tiffany favrile vase or bowl; the years of research and experiment had come to fruition and this astounding coloured glass in its many forms dazzled and entranced the public. But, by the end of the Great War, Art Nouveau was out of fashion and the man who had once led the way in artistic spheres found himself out of sympathy with the trend towards functional and rectilinear styles of art. Tiffany died in 1933, a lonely old man whose work was now completely disregarded. Thirty years later, the revival of Art Nouveau had begun, and continues to this day.

Above: The entrance to Samuel Bing's
shop, La Maison de l'Art Nouveau

To put Tiffany's art glass into perspective, we must go back to the
1890s. Emile Gallé's intricately-carved
and lavishly-decorated glassware that so
entranced Tiffany at the Paris Exposition of 1889 was much more than an
inspiration to the American. It was also
a personal triumph for Gallé after years
spent perfecting his art glass techniques;
yet, at the same time, it was symbolic of
the new direction which European arts
and crafts were to take.

The English Arts and Crafts Movement had pointed the way, attempting
to free the exponents of both fine and
applied arts from the shackles of 19th
century industrialization and the mass-

production of low-grade artefacts, but
they had reached back into the
past to achieve their aims through
simplification.

The new wave of artists and craftsmen wanted nothing to do with the past.
Instead they sought new and contemporary styles, virtually becoming a
movement that flaunted established
conventions and disdained the common-
place. They saw their role as creating an
entirely modern genre unrelated to anything that had gone before. The 1890s
thus became a period of intense experi-

mentation as painters and designers, architects and sculptors, writers and musicians, jewellers and typographers and glassmakers like Tiffany and Gallé searched for new ideas that matched their aspirations.

Like their arts and crafts predecessors they were often influenced by natural forms and by the understated beauty of Oriental art, particularly Japanese. But they totally rejected the realism that pervaded much of Victorian art and took refuge in symbolism, in which the artist tries to capture the *idea* behind the shape he is forming, in whatever medium. They interpreted what they felt, not what they saw.

This desire to express ideas through decorative forms probably began with painters in France, but they did not create the style: in a sense it developed more or less simultaneously and spontaneously all over Europe and soon spread to North America. Nor was it confined to paint on canvas: applied artists like Tiffany and Gallé and the sculptor Rodin rapidly embraced the new thinking.

Samuel Bing

It was known by different names in different countries, but in the mid-1890s the name that Samuel Bing chose when he remodelled his orientalist shop in the rue de Provence in Paris was finally adopted. Bing eagerly embraced the new art style in all its manifestations, gathered them together into one unified collection and called his shop La Maison de l'Art Nouveau.

Born in Hamburg, Bing became an influential patron of the arts and a specialist, in particular, of Japanese and Far Eastern styles: He was an internationally acknowledged and highly respected art critic, connoisseur, dealer and publisher when the new style began to emerge and thus a natural focus for its many forms. Other similar centres of Art Nouveau sprang up throughout Europe around this time and in France, in fact, there were two: the second was in Nancy where Gallé himself was the leader of an artistic coterie based on the glass industry of the region.

Bing's shop in Paris was undoubtedly one of the most important European centres for Art Nouveau. He himself described it as 'a meeting ground for all ardent young artists anxious to manifest the modernness of their tendencies'. But it was much more than a meeting place. Redesigned by the architect Louis Bonnier and the English painter Frank Brangwyn, it was the showcase *par excellence* for Art Nouveau art and artists. At the opening on 26 December 1895 Bing displayed glass by Gallé, jewellery by René Lalique, prints and drawings by Aubrey Beardsley and James Whistler, a wide selection of paintings by many European artists including Pissarro, Roussel, Ibels and Toulouse-Lautrec, together with furniture, sculpture (by Rodin among others) and posters.

Among this breathtaking assembly of artistic talent Louis Tiffany was treated as an equal: he was seen unequivocally as the foremost American exponent of Art Nouveau and from this point on, his international reputation was assured. Besides the ten stained-glass windows to

designs by French artists that Bing had commissioned after the 1889 Paris Exposition, Tiffany showed some 20 of his blown-glass pieces to considerable acclaim. He might have been inspired originally by Gallé some years earlier, but from that inspiration had sprung a totally original art form.

Aesthetically Tiffany's designs in glass were close to the European 'feel' of Art Nouveau, but they were never slavish copies of anything he saw in the Old World. They were seen as supreme examples of art glass in their own right, superior to most of what was being produced in Europe and, in fact, they

were probably the first artistic products of America to be copied in Europe. Leading Austrian and Bohemian glassmakers and designers, for instance, were among several manufacturers who produced Tiffany-style articles around the turn of the century.

Tiffany was doubtless flattered by such imitators although he was considerably less pleased by a rash of American copyists, some of them former employees of the Corona factory. He even sued one of his American imitators who produced iridescent glassware after 1904, but the lawsuit came to nothing as not even Tiffany could claim to have *invented* iridescence. It was a well known and established glassmaking technique and indeed the ancient glassware unearthed by archaeologists had taken on a patina akin to iridescence merely by lying in the soil.

Artistic Brilliance

What Tiffany did do in his art glass was to bring iridescence and other glassmaking techniques to a high level of artistic brilliance. The fact that he produced his Favrile glass articles in quantity does not detract in any way from their aesthetic quality. He was sometimes accused of betraying his artistic principles for commercialism, of creating a demand for art glass and then cashing in on that demand. Tiffany was disdainful of such criticism which he countered by insisting that the *raison d'être* for mass production at Corona was simply a wish to make his glassware available to the widest possible audience.

In one sense, of course, blown glass cannot be mass-produced: by its very nature each and every piece is unique, made by an individual act of creation. Tiffany and his artists produced the designs, McIlhiney and his chemists worked out the mixes and temperatures and the glassmakers provided the basic substance – but at the end of the day it was up to Arthur Nash and his glassblowing teams to take the glass and

Above: *Curling fern fronds inspired this unusual ceramic vase*

transform it into the glorious shapes that Tiffany presented to the world. Tiffany's genius was to turn all this individual creativity into mass-production by employing a large number of the finest designers and glassmakers and ensuring that they were all thoroughly versed in the styles and methods he had spent many years perfecting.

Each Tiffany art glass object was born, as any blown-glass piece is born, from a small, iridescent ball of glass from the furnace. Depending on the desired result, the glowing ball was then treated in an exact and often highly complex manner, following precise procedures worked out by Tiffany and his colleagues over days, weeks, and sometimes even months of careful experimentation.

Bing once explained:

'The workman charges (the ball of glass) at certain pre-arranged points with small quantities of glass of different textures and different colours, and in the operation is hidden the germ of the intended ornamentation. The little ball is then returned to the fire to be heated. Again it is subjected to a similar treatment (the process sometimes being repeated as many as twenty times) and, when all the different glasses have been combined and manipulated in different ways, and the article has been brought to its definite state as to form and dimensions . . . the motifs introduced into the ball when it was small have grown with the vase itself, but in differing proportions; they have lengthened or broadened, while each tiny ornament fills the place assigned to it in advance in the mind of the artist.'

Bing himself received some of the very first art glass pieces from Corona a year or so after production started in 1893. He was enraptured: '. . . after all the accomplishments of the Venetians, of Gallé and others, it is still possible to innovate, to utilize glass in a new way . . . with a surface that is like skin to the touch, silky and delicate'.

Press Reaction

After the 'world premier' in Paris in December 1895, Tiffany's art glass had its public launch in his own Fourth Avenue studios a few weeks later. Naturally the press was there, for Tiffany had been making news for some years; and if their comments seem oddly reticent this is perhaps not surprising for here were objects unlike anything most people had ever seen before. The glass was 'curious and entirely novel, both in color and texture,' wrote *The New York Times*, while the *Herald* found the variety of shades 'almost bewildering'. The *Commerical Advertiser* decided that the collection was 'a fine arts museum in itself, with all the attributes of form, beauty and design . . . the effects are spontaneous; there is no artificiality about them'.

If the journalists were cautiously guarded public reaction was considerably more decisive when the new glassware went on sale, although not all the comments were flattering. Many prominent Americans were still devoted to neo-gothic, neo-renaissance and neo-rococo styles of architecture and decor and they found the New Wave outrageous and Tiffany's art glass gaudy, even grotesque.

But many others welcomed the glass with almost ecstatic acclaim and started a craze for Art Nouveau; they felt that no self-respecting, arts-loving household should be without its Tiffany vase, bowl, lamp or other glassware and the sales boom began. As the Corona factory expanded output rose to prodigious heights and, while the craze lasted, the hard-worked teams of glassmakers were producing several thousand articles a year – every single one unique.

The fruits of Tiffany's research and experiments now began to flow from the factory in a bewildering variety of designs and finishes . . . the Cypriote and Antique ware simulating ancient and naturally corroded glass; the Lustre ware with its chemically-treated surfaces shining with dazzling iridescence or with a softer, pearl-like sheen; the roughly-textured Lava ware with flecks or shapes of lustred glass sparkling among the more sombre background shades; the translucent Reactive glass objects with their sinuous, organic or abstract internal patterns; Agate ware and marbleized glass with their scintillating striations; and the Carved glass with which Tiffany's craftsmen often rivalled Gallé, the master of the art of engraving and surface decorating.

Astounding Variety

Matching the finishes in their beauty and variety were the shapes that Tiffany's glass-blowers gave to the pieces – the spectacular Jack-in-the Pulpit vases, ornate gooseneck flasks, bulbous, gourd-shaped objects and incredibly slender flower-form vases, the Millefiore vases with their intricate, internal shapes and the Paperweight and Aquamarine pieces that sprang from the Millefiore technique. All were made in an unbelievable range of colours, for the Tiffany factory had hundreds of shades to draw on, from clear crystal to solid black through a rainbow spectrum of red and blue, green and yellow, purple

Above: *This double gourd vase was made circa 1900*

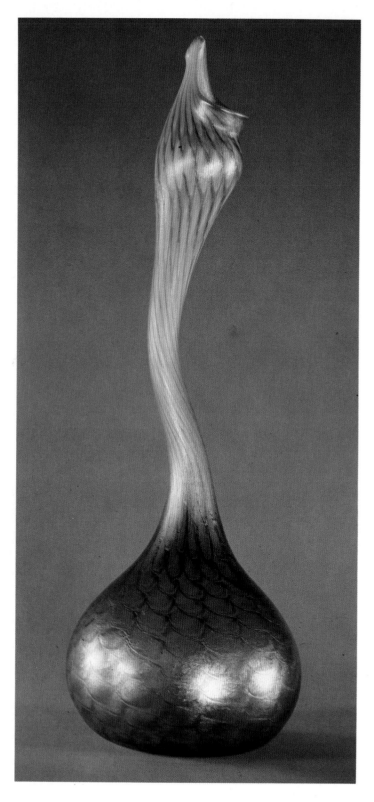

and gold, pink and violet, opal and ivory, and breathtaking combinations of these and many more.

There was another, more commercial aspect of Tiffany glassmaking during this period, for apart from the vases, bowls and other 'display' objects the company also produced highly-popular tableware, mostly in gold lustre but sometimes in deep blue iridescent glass (which was rarer and consequently commands much higher prices today). The matching pieces within each design style included a full range of glasses, from claret and champagne to liqueur and water glasses, together with such items as decanters, finger bowls and salt cellars. A variety of decorative patterns was produced including some that were engraved, usually with grapevine motifs on the inside or the outside of the objects.

Tiffany's Favrile art glass output reached its creative maturity during the early years of the 20th century. It waned as Art Nouveau gave way to other forms of modern art. Although the production of display items and tableware, stained-glass windows and mosaics, enamelware and jewellery, continued for varying lengths of time up to and even after the First World War, often resulting in stunningly beautiful creations to rival anything that had gone before, it rarely matched the overall innovative brilliance of the great years.

Left: *An iridescent Gooseneck vase. The inspiration for this design came from the ancient Persian rosewater sprinkler vases which Tiffany saw in the Middle East*

It may be that Tiffany himself lost that singleminded dedication to art glass that had brought his work to such majestic perfection around the turn of the century; and certainly he had other things on his mind. The death of his father in 1902 had given him the added responsibility of helping to manage the affairs of Tiffany and Co. The death of his second wife Louise two years later

was a devastating blow and he reacted as he had after his first wife's death by indulging in a highly theatrical lifestyle. In later years there were even hints of scandals, but they were always quickly hushed up.

Whatever the reasons the glass work began to attract unfavourable criticism. In one article in *The Craftsman* as early as 1903 the writer confessed to a 'deep disappointment' at Tiffany's current output. 'There is absolutely nothing to observe among these pieces – heavy, yet weak in form and with vivid, yet inharmonious colouring. We are indeed far from the exquisite specimens of Mr Tiffany's earlier manner . . .'

Ironically another problem may have stemmed from the enormous success of Tiffany Studios and the Corona factory for, wrapped up as he was in his other preoccupations, Tiffany had to rely more and more upon his designers to initiate new products which the glass-makers could produce quickly and in quantity for a still-clamouring market. He also lost some of his talented employees who eyed the market they had helped to create and left Corona to set up in competition. After 1902, Tiffany was also personally and deeply involved in one of his greatest artistic ventures — Laurelton Hall.

A decade or so after the completion of his New York town house he had bought and decorated a colonial-style family home and estate called The Briars on Long Island. Tiffany's interior for The Briars was far less ornate than the 72nd Street studio, perhaps because he was so involved at the time with his business affairs, or perhaps because of a general trend towards simplicity in interior decoration after the extravagance of previous commissions. But with Laurelton Hall the old, ostentatious Tiffany took over with a vengeance and it became an Art Nouveau showplace, one of the most publicized homes in America, the subject of lavishly illustrated features in many leading publications.

Tiffany himself designed the house, first demolishing an old hotel that had stood on the 580-acre, waterfront estate at Oyster Bay, Long Island. In its place a rambling, steel-framed and stucco-faced building was created round an enclosed central courtyard complete with a glass fountain and even a small stream. The house was 56.38 metres (185 ft) long and had 85 rooms (including 25 bathrooms) and an enormous, cavernous living room that was pure Art Nouveau in its fantastic, asymmetrical shape with a cavelike fireplace and iron-and-glass fixtures. In complete contrast a dining room that ran the full width of the house was light and airy, with floor-to-ceiling windows and simple and restrained furnishings and decor. The Tiffany works produced the finest glass and metal articles for the mansion, which also housed his priceless collection of art objects from many countries, cultures and centuries.

Laurelton Hall was an outward expression of Tiffany's conviction — sadly mistaken as it turned out — that he had become by this time the prime arbiter of cultural taste in the United States. He gave his first public lecture in October 1910 — on 'The Tasteful Use of Light and Color in Artificial Illumination' — but he wanted more than this. Teaching was for professors: he was a showman and craved a spectacle.

Perhaps influenced by the theatrical lifestyle he had often sought, but probably even more by a dawning realization that the tide of artistic taste was turning against him, he began to conceive the idea of staging extravagant events combining showmanship with aesthetics, to become P. T. Barnum and Samuel Bing rolled into one, to show the world that the Tiffany creative genius was still alive and well.

The first of these extraordinary happenings was staged in his New York Studios in February 1913 when several hundred guests enjoyed an Egyptian pageant, described by *The New York Times* as 'the most lavish costume fête ever seen in New York'. But the artistic purpose was drowned in a sea of champagne.

A year later Tiffany chartered a train and a fleet of cars to take 150 carefully-chosen guests to Laurelton Hall for a sumptuous banquet among surroundings that would prove that his artistic concepts were still valid. This, too, failed: the intellectuals at the party were more concerned with happenings 3,000 miles away — for war in Europe was by then inevitable.

For the third and last of these epic events Tiffany invited 200 guests to breakfast at his studio in February 1916 to celebrate his 68th birthday with a spectacular masque he called 'The Quest for Beauty'. He spared no expense (the lighting alone cost $15,000) in staging this amazing spectacle in which 45 characters acted, mimed and danced their way through a series of musical tableaux on the theme of 'art as the search for beauty and the effort to express it in many mediums throughout the ages'.

In a speech to his birthday guests Tiffany spoke of his own endless quest for beauty in all his works. In a tacit defence of Art Nouveau he poured scorn on the new style of art that was even then taking its place. 'The ''Modernists'' — as they are called for want of a better term — I mean Cubists, Futurists, etc — wander after curiosities of technique, vaguely hoping they may light on some invention which will make them famous. They do not belong to art, they are not artists; they are untrained inventors of processes of the arts'.

It was too late. Art Nouveau was dead, as dead as the millions littering the battlefields of Europe. The 'Modernists' had already won the day. Significantly, a day or two after Tiffany's first pageant three years before, an exhibition in New York had given

108

America its first glimpse of this new world of art with the works of Matisse and the Fauves, with Cubism and German Expressionism. Many American artists had also been represented at this exhibition but Tiffany was not among them. As it had so often in the past the

Below: *A reconstruction of the dining room at Laurelton Hall. Tiffany designed all the furniture; originally there were three dining tables; a large rectangular table was used for entertaining, and two smaller, octagonal tables were used at breakfast and lunchtime*

taste in art had moved inexorably on: years before it had taken him with it, this time it passed him by.

Almost as a last-ditch effort to halt this flow of events, to perpetuate his own style of art, Tiffany set up and funded the Louis C. Tiffany Foundation in 1918. It was a unique venture, a museum-school centred on Laurelton Hall and devoted to helping promising young artists by providing accommodation and studio facilities, teaching classes and recreational activities, and, above all, access to Tiffany's own extensive art collection. Students – who had to be Americans aged between 25 and 35 – were sponsored by art schools or recognized artists and were selected for their ability by a committee. It was

ultimately a highly successful experiment and Tiffany maintained a close and benevolent interest in the Foundation and its students until his death. In his declining years he had little else to remember with such affection.

When America entered the Great War in 1917 many of Tiffany's workers joined the forces or switched to war-work and production at both the Studios and the glass factory declined as a result. From this point on the end of Tiffany's dream was in sight, although it was to take a few more years before it finally faded away.

Below: A bookend from Tiffany Studios with a design inspired by a trailing vine on a green glass ground

In January 1920 Tiffany and Arthur Nash retired from active participation in the Corona glassworks, which changed its name to Louis C. Tiffany Furnaces Inc. with Arthur's son A. Douglas Nash in charge. The younger Nash continued to produce limited ranges of Favrile glassware and other articles and even reopened the enamelling department, but the exclusive, innovative days had gone. In 1928, irritated by what he saw as the increasing commercialism of the Corona works' output, Tiffany withdrew his financial support. The end came quickly and within a few months the factory closed. Favrile glass was dead.

Meanwhile Tiffany Studios had also been gently fading away, spending its declining years producing gift items and some stained glass. Its last major contract was for the decorating of the Presidential Palace in Havana, Cuba, in 1918; in 1925 it provided a stained-glass window for the Metropolitan Museum of Art in New York; and even as late as 1927 it filled an order from the White House for a green Aubusson rug incorporating the federal seal.

Winding Up

By this time, however, Tiffany was no longer involved and in fact the company had virtually ceased to exist; it was little more than a retail organization for the stocks still held. Joseph Briggs had been put in charge by Tiffany himself but it was a spectral company he ran, a ghost of its former self. In 1932 Briggs filed a petition for bankruptcy and even though the firm managed to struggle on

Above: *Joseph Briggs*

for a few more years this must have been a sad blow to the firm's creator.

It was only one of many disappointments that Tiffany suffered in his declining years. The Post-Impressionist Movement that had usurped Art Nouveau had left him stranded in an artistic time-warp of his own making and he was never able to come to terms with the harsh new styles, themselves the inevitable product of an embittered, postwar generation that looked on the extravagance of the recent past as decadence personified.

Geometric, rectilineal and functional, the new wave was worlds apart from the sinuous and sensuous styles that had gone before. Even the young students at the Tiffany Foundation, grateful though they doubtless were to their benefactor, were naturally more in sympathy with the newer art forms than the old; and although Tiffany enjoyed talking to them and studying their work he was often puzzled by it. But he never criticized them openly; he simply smiled gently, talked about the importance of beauty in art and said that painting should not 'hurt the eye'. It was a telling remark.

Tiffany was not totally ignored during the 1920s. He was still a famous American and his views were often sought on a variety of topics by news reporters and commentators; but his glassware was no longer in public fashion and the arts world in general largely disregarded his work as irrelevant.

This neglect reinforced Tiffany's isolation. His extrovert exterior had always cloaked an innate shyness and reticence and these now became his dominant traits. He had little contact with his family or his former employees and his only companion was an Irish woman called Sarah Hanley, who had gone to Laurelton Hall to nurse him through an illness and stayed on to beome his protégée.

Tiffany built her a house on the Oyster Bay estate and taught her to paint, and together this odd couple – the elderly, eccentric American millionaire and the simple Irish woman – would visit the factory and studio and the occasional exhibition or wander around the Laurelton estate, painting pictures of flowers and of each other. Sarah was with him until the end.

The end came on 17 January 1933, a month before his 85th birthday, when Tiffany died at his New York home, mourned by Sarah and a handful of loyal friends but scarcely at all by his family,

his employees, his erstwhile fellow artists or the fickle public, which by then had largely forgotten him. His death snapped one of the final links in the tenuous chain that bound the 'thirties to the days of Art Nouveau: Gallé and Rodin, Toulouse-Lautrec and Beardsley and many other masters had all died some years before. The style they had created had died with them and Tiffany's art glass, too, followed the genre into a long, dark period of obscurity and neglect.

To Joseph Briggs went the thankless task of disposing of the remainder of the glassware. Details of the long association between the two men are scarce but it is certain that the millionaire New Yorker had a high regard for his one-time English apprentice. Tiffany's grandson, William T. Lusk, who was president of Tiffany and Co from 1955 to 1967, recalled in a letter, 'I gather that Louis had complete faith in Joseph Briggs and entrusted the management of his company to him after his death'. In an obituary on Tiffany in February 1933 *The Upholsterer and Interior Decorator* spoke of '. . . Joseph Briggs, who for forty-three years has worked side by side with Mr Tiffany and conscientiously reflected the Tiffany spirit . . .'.

Some reports suggest that after Tiffany's death the entire stock of glass and other art ware, valued at $600,000, was given to Briggs as a gift. This is unlikely for what Briggs actually did was to arrange for the stock of Tiffany

Right: *A Maple leaf table lamp with a particularly elaborate base*

Above: Sulphur Crested Cockatoos, *the glass mosaic exhibition piece in the Haworth Art Gallery, Accrington, Lancashire*

Studios to be auctioned. Details of these sales, too, are scant: they were evidently held in several places over several years but the pieces achieved very low prices and there is evidence to suggest that Briggs consigned some stock to the rubbish tips of New York. Certainly many previously proud owners of classic Tiffany glassware threw it out (no doubt to their considerable regret in view of what happened a generation later!)

Joseph Briggs had also assembled his own private collection of Tiffany art glass over the years. In 1933, three years before his death, he returned to England for the last time, gave half of his collection to relatives and friends, and presented the remainder – totalling over 120 pieces including 67 high-quality vases, 45 tiles and eight mosaics – to the Corporation of Accrington. Quite what the town fathers thought of the gift is not recorded: they were coping with the immense problems of an area left seriously depressed by the slump in the cotton trade, with a legacy of Victorian slums and worn-out amenities, and a third of the local workforce unemployed. Briggs' gift of unfashionable and derided Art Nouveau glassware that belonged to an affluent and totally alien society of thirty years before must have seemed almost irrelevant. Nonetheless it was displayed in the town museum and later transferred to the Haworth Art Gallery. But to the handful of American connoisseurs who kept faith with Art Nouveau and Tiffany glass during the years of obscurity, this important collection was totally unknown.

Meanwhile the Tiffany Foundation was also struggling with its legacy from the past. In 1942 a marine research unit took over Laurelton Hall and after the war the Foundation obtained legal sanction to break the provisions of Tiffany's Trust, sell off the estate they could no longer afford to maintain, and use the proceeds to fund further art scholarships.

In 1946 the entire contents of the

Hall, the results of a lifetime of devoted collecting by Louis Tiffany, were sold at auction for a fraction of their original value. They included many items of Tiffany art glass marked 'A Coll', which showed that they had been chosen by Tiffany for his own personal collection. A few years later the Hall itself, together with four acres of land fronting on to Oyster Bay, was sold for a mere $10,000. Forty years before the estate had been conservatively valued at nearly $2 million.

Revival and Reappraisal

In 1957 Laurelton Hall was destroyed by fire, but instead of marking the end of the Tiffany era, it coincided with the first faint flutterings of an Art Nouveau revival that were even then stirring in the art world. Within a few years a complete reappraisal of the entire genre was destined to send values soaring. In the 1946 sale of around 600 items from Laurelton Hall at the Parke-Bernet Galleries in New York some of the finest examples of Tiffany art glass raised almost derisory amounts. A signed piece marked 'Favrile glass flower vase, cylindrical with pinched neck and elongated foliage decoration in a golden and flame iridescent ground' sold for $20. The top price of the sale was reached by 'six Favrile glass finger bowls with trays . . . invested with a golden rainbow iridescence'. They realized $180. A pair of 'millefiore aquamarine glass spheres, irregularly shaped with millefiore marine decoration' made $75. Two 76 cm (30 inch) diameter chandeliers from Laurelton Hall sold for $50.

A year later and 3,000 miles away the curator at the Haworth Art Gallery in Accrington had his Tiffany collection valued for insurance: the total for more than 120 pieces was £1,500. Many Favrile glass vases were rated at £5 and £10, some of the finest examples of Tiffany tiles in existence at as little as £2 or £3 each, and a stunning, multi-coloured, opaque glass mosaic of two cockatoos was appraised at just £50.

Today that cockatoo mosaic is valued at £130,000; but even by the mid-1960s the price of Tiffany glass had started to move up smartly. Robert Koch in his *International Antiques Yearbook* article reported that in 1946 a set of four Favrile vases had sold for just $70 the set. In a 1966 sale at the Parke-Bernet Galleries the same four came up again. Three of them made over $2,500 each. The fourth, a mere 9 cm ($3\frac{1}{2}$ inches) tall and described as 'ochre and blue vase, urn form and having a wreath of slightly incised iridescent blue, ochre and brown leaves and vines at the shoulder, on an iridescent blue and brown ground' brought the highest price of the sale, an astonishing $3,250. In contrast to the two Tiffany chandeliers that had made $50 the pair in 1946, Parke-Bernet sold a peacock feather lamp for $2,300 in 1967 while a dragonfly lamp, that had cost $185 brand new in 1928, realized $2,250 in 1967.

The revival of Tiffany matched the reappraisal of Art Nouveau itself, starting as early as 1949 with the opening of a gallery devoted to the genre at the Museum of Modern Art in New York; and within a decade the renaissance was well under way. It was spurred on in the 1950s by the advent of Abstract Expressionism in the United States, spearheaded by Jackson Pollock and Robert Motherwell who championed Tiffany as an early exponent of pure form and colour in art, expressed through free design.

Not surprisingly the number of collectors increased enormously, a factor that is reflected in the spiralling prices for Tiffany art glass at this time. Some American dealers and enthusiasts followed the faint trail to Accrington and tried to buy the Briggs collection; but the town was by then fully aware of the importance of its treasures and refused to sell. Today the Briggs bequest, estimated at around £1 million, is the largest collection of its kind in Europe and from the quality viewpoint considered to be among the finest in the world.

Soaring Prices

By November 1970 the *Financial Times* in London was able to put the whole revival into perspective in a major review of the art market. It cited as examples a Tiffany glass and bronze Dragonfly lamp that had sold for £804 in 1967 and £2,917 only three years later; and a Gooseneck vase in the Persian style that had made just £11 in 1946, £155 in 1967 and £340 in 1970.

In its wide-ranging survey the *Financial Times* reported:

The real market in Art Nouveau is less than 10 years old. Specialist sales, which are now held regularly in Paris, London and New York, did not take place much before 1965 and the general level of prices before that date was so low as to have little or no relevance to the sums which have been paid during the past three or four years.

It is no denegation of Art Nouveau to say that it is one small area of the art market which has been "rediscovered" in recent years to meet the demands of an enormously increased body of collectors of works of art in general. After almost 60 years of neglect it was a rediscovery that was long overdue.

At the beginning of the 1960s, Art Nouveau was the province of a small band of dedicated and – so they were then considered – eccentric collectors. Today the reverse is true – no style or type of art has such a wide appeal. Not only is this due to its highly decorative quality but also to the fact that it is still relatively inexpensive to form a representative collection.

One of the most important subsections of Art Nouveau is Tiffany glass, produced by Louis Comfort Tiffany in America. This type of glass . . .is greatly in demand among American collectors and for this reason – quite apart from its high quality – is one of the most expensive types of Art Nouveau.

The price levels attained by the pieces in the (1966) sale were extremely high and in many cases have remained constant ever since. When the piece is not in the very top bracket, however, there has been a considerable rise between 1966 and 1970. A fine tapering lobed vase fetched £536 in 1966 as opposed to the £1,667 made by a very similar example in 1970.

What has happened since 1966, therefore, is that the very best and most expensive examples have risen the least and the more modest pieces, in the sense of both quality and price, have risen the most. The 1966 sale had the effect of generating tremendous interest in the collecting of Tiffany glass and since that sale, the greater availability of middle-range examples has meant that they have been the focus of the most concentrated buying. Really superb, rare and expensive pieces are usually bought as the summation of an already existing collection. . .'

Louis Comfort Tiffany would have been pleased and flattered by this revival of interest in his works, but not unduly surprised that people were prepared to pay high prices for even modest examples. He had never felt the need to sacrifice quality on the altar of popularity and had remained true to his ideals in all his spheres of endeavour, as a painter, as a decorator and above all as the creator of art glass.

As Tiffany himself once said, '. . . I have always striven to fix beauty in wood or stone, or glass or pottery, in oil or water-color, by using whatever seemed fittest for the expression of beauty; that has been my creed and I see no reason to change it . . . '.

Above: *A slender baluster-shaped Paperweight vase. The interior is lightly covered with gold iridescence*

REFERENCE SECTION

MUSEUMS AND PUBLIC COLLECTIONS

Owing to the sheer volume of production by the Tiffany glassworks and studios, it is impossible to give an exhaustive list of all the museums, galleries, churches and public buildings with examples of Louis Tiffany's work. Indeed, many of his great stained-glass windows and mosaics in private houses were either destroyed or dismantled by owners who found them too ostentatious for modern taste. Much of Tiffany's work has found its way into private collections and is not available for public inspection. However, the following museums all contain examples of Tiffany's work.

France
Musée des Arts Decoratifs
107 rue de Rivoli
Paris 75001

Although this museum has a collection of Tiffany glass, it is not on general view and can only been seen by appointment.

Great Britain
Haworth Art Gallery
Accrington
Lancashire

A collection of 130 pieces, making it the largest collection in Europe and one of the finest in the world. The collection was presented to the town of Accrington by Joseph Briggs who worked with Louis Tiffany for almost forty years.

Victoria and Albert Museum
South Kensington
London SW7

A collection of about 15 pieces of glass.

Below: This iridescent Millefiore vase can be seen at the Haworth Art Gallery, Accrington, Lancashire

United States of America
Museums and Galleries

Chrysler Museum Institute of Glass
Olney Road and Mowbray Arch
Norfolk
Virginia 23510

An important collection with over 250 pieces. It includes glass and pottery vases, lamps, mosaics and tableware.

Corning Museum of Glass
Museum Way
Corning
New York 13830

An interesting collection including stained-glass windows, lamps and metalwork.

Metropolitan Museum of Art
Fifth Avenue at 82nd Street
New York
New York 10028

The museum's collection began with 56 items donated by Henry Havemeyer, a client of Tiffany's and probably the first bona fide collector of Tiffany art glass.

Morse Gallery of Art
133 East Welbourne Avenue
Winter Park
Florida 32789

The 4,000 items amassed by the Charles Hosmer Morse Foundation make up the most important collection of Tiffany material in the world.

Stained-Glass Windows & Mosaics

A comprehensive list of stained-glass windows appears in *Tiffany Windows* by Alastair Duncan (Thames & Hudson, London and Simon & Schuster Inc., New York) which is a must for all serious students of Tiffany. Listed below are the locations of some particularly interesting examples:

Mark Twain Memorial
351 Farmington Avenue
Hartford
Connecticut 06105

Episcopal Church of the Incarnation
Madison Avenue and 35th Street
New York City

Madison Square Presbyterian Church
New York City

Collegiate Reformed Dutch Church
Second Avenue and 7th Street
New York City

Old Blandford Church
Petersburgh
Virginia

Dream Garden mosaic
Curtis Center
Independence Square
Philadelphia

American Red Cross Headquarters
Assembly Hall
Washington
D.C.

HALLMARKS

All Tiffany's favrile glass was marked with the signature L.C. Tiffany or L.C.T. The very first pieces from the Corona glasshouse came with numbered paper labels and later this same number was also engraved on the glass. In the years 1892–3 pieces were numbered from 1–9999, thereafter the prefix A was used for the next 9999 pieces, followed by B and so on. After the letter Y, pieces were then given a number followed by a suffix letter. The list below shows when the different date letters appeared.

1–9999 1892–3	Prefixes W and Y 1905
Prefixes A and B 1894	Suffix A 1906
Prefixes C and D 1895	Suffix B 1907
Prefixes E and F 1896	Suffix C 1908
Prefixes G and H 1897	Suffix D 1909
Prefixes I and J 1898	Suffix E 1910
Prefixes K and L 1899	Suffix F 1911
Prefixes M and N 1900	Suffix G 1912
Prefixes O and P 1901	Suffix H 1913
Prefixes Q and R 1902	Suffix I 1914
Prefixes S and T 1903	Suffix J 1915
Prefixes U and V 1904	Suffix K 1916
	Suffix L 1917
	Suffix M 1918
	Suffix N 1919
	Suffix O 1920
	Suffix P 1921
	Suffix Q 1922
	Suffix R 1923
	Suffix S 1924
	Suffix T 1925
	Suffix U 1926
	Suffix V 1927
	Suffix W 1928

Left: The base of a marbleized decanter (diameter 6 cm ($2\frac{1}{4}$ inches) showing the favrile trademark and the inscription L.C. Tiffany D 947 (circa 1895). The price label is authentic, but this decanter is now worth about £4,000

There were four more prefixes. A small o is thought to denote pieces made for a special order; an X designates an experimental piece and Ex or Exhibition Piece is precisely what it says. A piece marked A-Coll was made for Tiffany's own collection.

Glass left the glasshouse bearing a sticker on the base with the favrile trademark. There were several versions of this sticker but very few still exist.

Lamps

All Tiffany's leaded lampshades carry a small copper tab soldered on to the inside of the shade, usually at the bottom of the rim. It bears the words TIFFANY STUDIOS NEW YORK and sometimes there is a number as well.

Lamp bases made before 1900 have the monogram TGDCo (Tiffany Glass and Decorating Company) and a serial number on the base; those made in 1900–2 carry the words TIFFANY STUDIOS NEW YORK, and the TGDCo monogram and a serial number. In 1902 the monogram was dropped and pattern numbers were used instead of serial numbers. Lamp bases made in 1912–28 carry the monogram LCT and the mark LOUIS C. TIFFANY FURNACES INC. FAVRILE.

Above: *The base of a Cameo vase (diameter 8.9 cm ($3\frac{1}{2}$ inches), bearing the favrile mark in the centre of the pontil. This piece was made circa 1907*
Below: *The base of another Cameo vase (diameter 6.5 cm ($2\frac{1}{2}$ inches)) with the favrile label in metallic green and gold. W 7842 denotes piece made circa 1905*

BIBLIOGRAPHY

Books

AMAYA, Mario
Tiffany Glass
Studio Vista, London, 1967

ARMITAGE, E.L.
Stained Glass
Charles T. Branford Co., Newton,
    Mass., 1959

ARWAS, Victor
Glass: Art Nouveau to Art Deco
Academy Editions, London, 1977

ARWAS, Victor
Tiffany
Academy Editions, London, 1979

BANGERT, Albrecht
Glass: Art Nouveau and Art Deco
Cassell Ltd, London, 1979

DE KAY, Charles (anonymous author)
The Art Work of Louis C. Tiffany
Doubleday, Page & Co., New York,
    1914

DUNCAN, Alastair
Tiffany at Auction
Rizzoli, New York, 1981

DUNCAN, Alastair
Tiffany Windows
Thames and Hudson, London, 1980

FREEMAN, Larry
Iridescent Glass
Century House, Watkins Glen, N.Y.

GARNER, Philippe
Art Nouveau for Collectors,
Hamlyn, London, 1974

GARNER, Philippe
Glass 1900: Gallé, Tiffany, Lalique
Thames and Hudson, London, 1979

GROVER, Ray and Lee
Art Glass Nouveau
Rutland, Vermont, 1968

KOCH, Robert H. (Ed.) S. Bing
Artistic America, Tiffany Glass and
    Art Nouveau
Cambridge, Mass., 1970

KOCH, Robert H.
Louis C. Tiffany — Rebel in Glass
Crown Publishers Inc., New York,
    1964

KOCH, Robert H.
Louis C. Tiffany's Glass, Bronzes,
    Lamps
A Complete Collector's Guide
Crown Publishers Inc., New York,
    1971

LEE, Ruth Webb
Nineteenth Century Art Glass
M. Barrows & Co., New York, 1949

McKEAN, Hugh
The 'Lost' Treasures of Louis
    Comfort Tiffany
Doubleday & Co., New York, 1980

MEHLMAN, Felice
The Illustrated Guide to Glass
Peerage Books, London, 1985

NEUSTADT, Egon
The Lamps of Tiffany,
New York, 1970

PAUL, Tessa
The Art of Louis Comfort Tiffany
Quintet Publishing Ltd., London,
    1987

REVI, Albert Christian
American Art Nouveau Glass
Thomas Nelson & Sons, New York,
    1968

SAARINEN, Aline
The Proud Possessors
Random House Inc., New York, 1958

SELZ, Peter and CONSTANTINE,
    Mildren (Ed)
Art Nouveau: Art and Design at the
    Turn of the Century
Secker of Warburg, London, 1975

WATKINS, Lura Woodside
American Glass and Glassmaking
Chanticleer Press, New York, 1950

WHEELER, Candace
Principles of Decoration
Doubleday, Page & Co., New York,
    1903

Catalogues

Exhibition of L'Art Nouveau, S. Bing
Grafton Galleries, London
Introduction by S. Bing
London, 1899

The Tiffany Collection of the
    Chrysler Museum at Norfolk
Paul E. Doros
Norfolk, 1978

Treasures of Tiffany
Hugh F. McKean
Museum of Science & Industry,
    Chicago, 1982

INDEX

ACKNOWLEDGEMENTS

The authors and publishers would like to thank the individuals and organisations listed below for their kind permission to reproduce the photographs in this book:

Trevor Adams Photography page 120, 121; The Bridgeman Art Library 12, 30, 81, 95, 103, 110; The Chrysler Museum Institute of Glass, Norfolk, VA, Gift of Walter P Chrysler, JR, 26, 47 right, 84, 86, 100, 104; Tom Crane/The Kevin F Donohoe Company 66–67; Alastair Duncan 2, 9, 11, 19, 37, 48, 50, 52, 54, 55, 57, 59, 60, 61, 63, 64, 74, 77, 78, 83, 85, 88, 89, 96, 113; Sonia Halliday 15; Geoffrey Proctor/Haworth Art Gallery 4, 31, 32, 33, 34, 35 top left, top centre, top right and bottom, 38 top and bottom, 39 top and bottom, 40 top and bottom, 41 left and right, 42, 43, 44 left, centre and right, 45 left and right, 46, 47 left, 62, 79, 91 left and right, 111, 114, 117, 118, 120, 121 top and bottom; Michael Holford 16, 17, 28, 29; Institut Français d'Architecture 98; The Charles Hosmer Morse Museum of American Art, Winter Park, Florida, through the courtesy of the Charles Hosmer Morse Foundation 6, 14, 18, 69, 71, 72, 73, 87, 92, 93, 94 top and bottom, 101, 105, 106, 108–109; The New York Historical Society 8, 21, 22, 90; Mark Twain Memorial Hartford, CT, 24–25.

The publishers would also like to thank MaryBeth McCaffrey, Alastair Duncan's Assistant and Ann Gerken at The Charles Hosmer Morse Foundation for their help and cooperation in submitting photographic material, and the Chrysler Museum Institute of Glass for their assistance with information on the dating system for Tiffany's Favrile glass.

In addition the publishers would like to thank the *Financial Times* and Sotheby's for their kind permission to publish the extract from the *Financial Times* of 21 November 1970 quoted on pages 116–117.

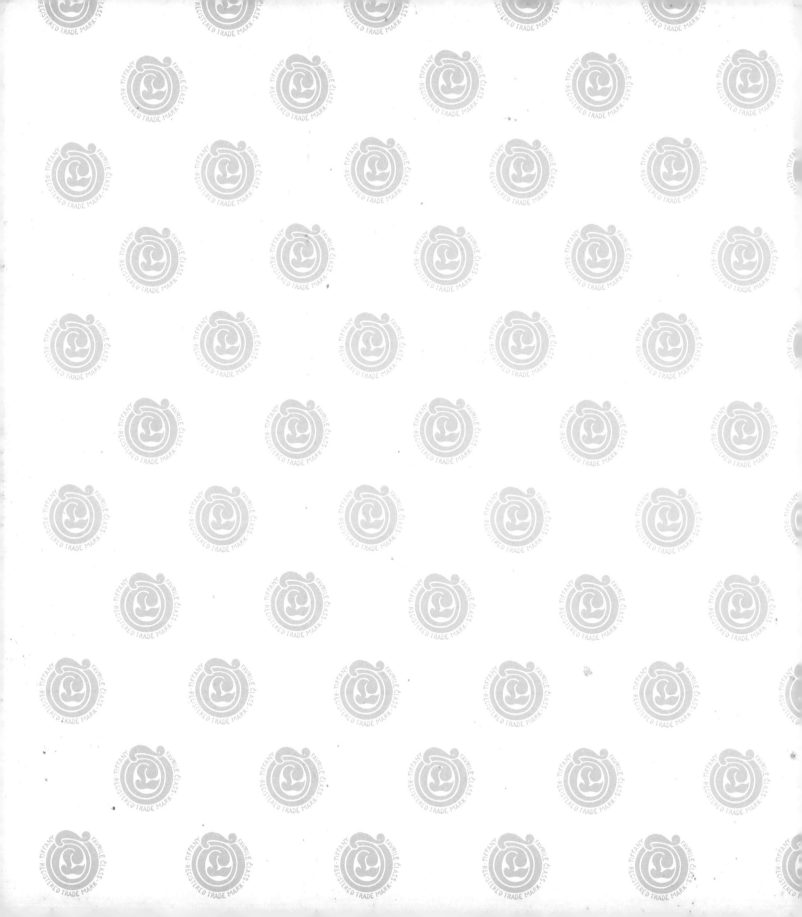